The Mathematics Teacher's Handbook

Also available from Continuum

Getting the Buggers to Add Up (2nd edition) – Mike Ollerton
100+ Ideas for Teaching Mathematics – Mike Ollerton
50 Mathematics Lessons – Colin Foster
Resources for Teaching Mathematics 14-16 – Colin Foster
Teaching and Learning Mathematics (2nd edition) – Marilyn Nickson
The Secondary Teacher's Handbook (2nd edition) – Lyn Overall and Margaret Sangster
The Ultimate Supply Teacher's Handbook – Deborah Hughes
The Art and Design Teacher's Handbook – Susie Hodge
The Business Studies Teacher's Handbook – Margaret Gane
The Citizenship Teacher's Handbook – Kate Brown and Stephen Fairbrass
The English Language Teacher's Handbook - Joanna Baker and Heather Westrup
The English Teacher's Handbook - Helena Ceranic
The Geography Teacher's Handbook – Brin Best
The History Teacher's Handbook – Neil Smith
The RE Teacher's Handbook – Cavan Wood

Available from Network Continuum

Even Better Mathematics – Afzal Ahmed and Honor Williams
Pocket PAL: Building Learning in Mathematics – Stephanie Prestage, Els De Geest and Anne Watson

The Mathematics Teacher's Handbook

Mike Ollerton

continuum

Continuum International Publishing Group

The Tower Building
11 York Road
London, SE1 7NX

80 Maiden Lane, Suite 704
New York
NY 10038

www.continuumbooks.com

British Library Cataloguing-in-Publication Data
A catalogue record for this book is available from the British Library.

ISBN: 9781847060112 (paperback)

Library of Congress Cataloguing-in-Publication Data
A catalog record for this book is available from the Library of Congress.

Typeset by BookEns Ltd, Royston, Herts.
Printed and bound in Great Britain by

Contents

Acknowledgements

I did not think I had any further writing left in me post *Getting the Buggers to Add Up*; however, Christina Garbett at Continuum proved me wrong and I thank her a great deal for doing so and for seeing this book through from conception to birth ... talking of which ... The other person I must thank is Ali Cooper, my lovely partner. Ali, academically, picked me up by the scruff of the neck and encouraged me to start studying with the Open University at age 35; thus the beginning of my learning to write – hugs and kisses aplenty. Finally, I have been most fortunate to meet and work with dozens of people who have given me much to ponder on, to reflect upon, to celebrate and to question regarding issues about learning and teaching mathematics; if you should read this, you will know who you are, and thank you.

Introduction

I have chosen to begin this book with an anecdote told to me by a young teacher in the third year of his teaching career. My reason for retelling the anecdote is because I believe it captures a great deal of what teaching and learning is fundamentally about: relationships. The event focuses upon the affective (emotional) and professional domain of relationships between teachers, and between teachers and students. I mention this because teachers and students also engage in cognitive (conceptual) relationships with different disciplines and I develop this later in this introduction. The context for the anecdote is a head of year (Mr P) remonstrating with a Year 10 student, Sam, for missing another teacher's history lesson (Mr J). The anecdote is retold by Mr J.

> I was starting to feel uncomfortable when Mr P seemed to be going over the top in remonstrating with Sam over his behaviour; it began to feel like it was turning into a 'character assassination' and this was definitely not a part of my approach to teaching. However, I had been requested to witness this telling-off so all I could do was wait until the deluge was over and try to maintain a professional stance. At one point in the tirade Mr P said:
>
> *'And what have you got to say to Mr J for skiving his lesson?'*
>
> *'Sorry, Sir,'* said Sam to Mr J.
>
> When it appeared the telling-off was about to reach its conclusion Sam said to Mr P, *'Please can I have a private word with Mr J before the next lesson?'*
>
> Almost begrudgingly Mr P agreed and presently left the scene.
>
> *'I really am sorry for missing your lesson, Sir.'*
>
> At hearing this Mr J was relieved that what he had thought was a sound relationship with Sam had not seemingly been too fractured by events.
>
> *'You see,'* continued Sam, *'I thought I was skiving off English.'*

In this short anecdote we can see many layers of what teaching is largely about; the annoyance and frustrations of one teacher, the delicate balance needing to be exhibited by another who had to be seen to be supporting a colleague, despite a feeling of unease at that colleague's way of handling a situation. Then, of course, there was the unexpected response from a student bringing a complex and delicate situation to an amusing close. Here we can begin to see relationships involved in this one small event in the lives of two teachers, one student and another teacher, of English, to whom Mr J chose not to retell the anecdote. Some of us would pay good money to see such drama being acted out on the stage or the screen.

Relationships, however, as I mention above, are not only of the affective or emotional type being developed and played out in the hundreds of interactions that take place each day between colleagues and with students. The other kind of relationship is the cognitive. What teachers attempt to do is to use their relationship with their subject and their relationships with students in order to help students form their own relationship, intentionally a positive one, with the subject. The complexity for teachers is that they cannot force students to have a positive relationship with their subject; they can only provide the opportunities for students. However, teachers have a massive impact on which subjects their students like and choose to pursue to higher levels and this is what this book, therefore, is all about. Before introducing each chapter, I intend to develop the notion of a cognitive relationship with mathematics and what the implications are for teachers seeking to promote their students' formation of a positive relationship with mathematics.

'Mathematics is fun!'

I have seen this proclamation posted on very many classroom walls. What exactly this phrase means or what students are meant to understand by it is anyone's guess. How anyone feels about mathematics, like beauty, lies in the 'eyes' of the beholder. Mathematics is certainly not described as 'fun' by the vast majority of the hundreds of adults I have discussed this issue with, many of them worryingly training to teach mathematics. Mathematics, however, can become fun, though I prefer to use the word 'enjoyable'.

I invite you to consider for a moment what makes anything enjoyable. Perhaps you might like to jot a few responses down in order to analyse what lies at the heart of your enjoyment of something. When you have completed this list you may wish to consider what you think makes the learning of mathematics enjoyable.

OK, I admit this notion of leaving a blank page in a book where the reader is invited to make some notes is not of my invention. The same idea appears on page 66 of *Teaching as a Subversive Activity* (1969) by Postman and Weingartner, an excellent publication offering teachers, advisors and politicians much to contemplate.

To continue I suggest enjoyment is, in part, arrived at by becoming evermore skilled with something or at ease with somebody. Enjoyment is gained by feelings of harmony, perhaps with another person or with the natural environment, maybe when walking the fells or cycling on the byroads and back roads. So it is in a mathematics classroom. Students enjoy learning mathematics as a result of achieving success in this venture; by being empowered as mathematicians. The more confident any student becomes, the more competent they become. Achievement breeds confidence, confidence breeds competence and competence causes enjoyment. The higher any student's achievement is with mathematics, the more they 'should' enjoy mathematics. Basing the effective learning of mathematics upon achievement is, therefore, what this book is about. It is about teaching and learning mathematics through problem-solving and problem-posing approaches.

In each chapter I weave several ideas for the mathematics classroom. My aim for doing so is to keep curriculum development uppermost. Indeed, it is only by working on some mathematics that we can contemplate how an idea might a) be utilized in our teaching and, more importantly, b) what the reasons are, the pedagogic implications, for using any task in our teaching. Each of the ideas I provide are intended to engage you in these two aims. As an example, or as a starter for lots more ideas, I offer the following task, which I have used in KS2 classrooms and with a bit of a tweak would be suitable also for KS3 classrooms. The task is based upon giving pupils a copy of the following grid (I use either A4 or A5 size grids copied on brightly coloured card).

100	10	1
H	T	U
0	0	0
0	0	0

I also give pupils, working in pairs, two numbers such as 2 and 5 on small pieces of card, which will fit on top of the spaces currently occupied by zeros. The task, therefore, is to place the two numbers on the grid, by covering up two of the zeros and then to carry out an addition calculation. The exploration is for pupils, working in pairs, to find all the different totals that could be made. I initially chose the numbers 2 and 5 so as not to 'bridge' a 10. Immediately in using such a problem I have engaged with certain pedagogic issues:

- Getting pupils to work together in a pair enables discussion and mutual support.
- I have provided a task to which there are a number of possible solutions.
- I am getting the class working as quickly as possible using minimum teacher input.
- My teaching role has already been partly carried out via the preparation of the grids and my plans to offer such a problem.
- I want the pupils to explore something that enables them to engage with a fundamentally important mathematical structure head-on, that is the place value system.
- Pupils will be using and applying some mathematics they can already do to find out something more than they currently know. This is about access.

Each of these pedagogic implications will be explored further. As with all other ideas, tasks and problems described in this book, I develop a commentary for using the task and the pedagogic implications. While this task is by no means completely open-ended (that is there are exactly nine different answers to be found), the task can be opened up as follows:

- Pupils can be encouraged to try to explain why they think they have found all the possible answers.
- They might be asked to place the numbers in order from smallest to largest, then find the differences between consecutive pairs of answers.
- What happens if two numbers are chosen that when added together bridge 10?
- What happens if we have a grid with more or fewer than three columns?
- What happens if we place three digits on a grid with three rows of zeros?

A further essential element in this task is about recognizing which zeros are redundant as this helps pupils further develop their understanding of the place value system.

A development of the same idea could be to offer pupils the following grid, where a decimal point appears.

10	1	●	1/10
T	U	●	t
0	0	●	0
0	0	●	0

Clearly all the answers that can be found on the earlier grid can be mapped onto all the answers on the decimal grid. The key difference is that each of the first set of answers will be (or should be) ten times greater than the equivalent values on the decimal grid. Thus, by having both grids and both sets of answers, comparisons can be made both ways between grids; that is multiplying by 10 when mapping answers from the TU●t grid to the HTU grid and dividing by 10 when mapping answers from the HTU grid to the TU●t grid.

To make this task more appropriate for KS3 students we can provide a grid that contains four columns with two of the columns after the decimal point. Again the same problem can be set up for students to seek to solve.

10	1	●	1/10	1/100
T	U	●	t	H
0	0	●	0	0
0	0	●	0	0

Without further ado, I shall offer the following synopses of the next ten chapters. Chapter 1 is intended for trainee teachers and an experienced teacher may wish to skip over this. However, the chapter does contain ideas that can be used in any classroom, whether you are a trainee teacher or an experienced practitioner. It mainly considers what might be one of the more challenging and possibly 'scariest' events in a trainee teacher's life, that of going 'solo' for the first time. I consider ways of trying to make this event a positive and fulfilling one.

Chapter 2 is about classroom culture and invites you to consider what, at its best, you would like your classroom to sound, look and feel like. I explore not just how the culture is created by the teacher, but also what the elements might be in order to help pupils develop as mathematicians; the learning culture.

Chapter 3 asks you to consider the question: 'We teach what we believe but do we believe what we teach?' In this chapter I ask you to revisit some of your own experiences as a learner of mathematics when you were at school. The intention is to examine some of your formative mathematical experiences and then to consider what impact these experiences can have upon your conception of the teaching of mathematics. Considering our teachers' approaches to the way they organized their classrooms, what worked well and what did not is one way of helping us determine how we want our pupils to experience mathematics.

Chapter 4 is about learning mathematics through exploration and about encouraging pupils to see themselves as explorers. It is also aligned to the notion of 'discovery learning' as defined by the Plowden Report published in 1967, another worthy educational tome from the 1960s. In this chapter I consider some situations and ideas that can be offered to pupils to explore and, as a consequence, engage in mathematical thinking in order to make sense of mathematics. Sense making is everything but it is only pupils who can make sense of what they are learning; we, as teachers, cannot do the learning for them.

Chapter 5 considers the balance between teaching and learning; developing key themes about who is doing the work and minimizing the traditional role of the teacher as a teller of information or an explainer of algorithms. In this chapter I challenge the notion of someone who wants to 'pass on their knowledge', and instead consider how to maximize pupils' responsibilities for thinking mathematically. This chapter contains a range of ideas suitable for a wide age range of pupils, as well as tasks that can be worked on collaboratively, and extending ideas even to revising for examinations.

Chapter 6 is based upon a seminal article written by Alan Wigley from a journal of the Association of Teachers of Mathematics (ATM), *Mathematics Teaching* (MT141, 1992). The chapter considers what might be considered a two polar models to teaching mathematics, the 'path-smoothing' model and the 'challenging' model. I consider times when I have found both of these models appropriate for specific situations.

Chapter 7 focuses upon assessment, or more accurately the integration of assessment practices into 'normal' teaching and learning that takes place in classrooms. I describe a project called 'Assessing Pupils' Progress', devised and piloted by the Qualifications and Curriculum Authority (QCA). I consider the effectiveness of the APP approach and its potential for impacting upon curriculum development in schools. Also in this chapter I revisit a 100 per cent teacher-assessed GCSE scheme I was involved in as a head of department and consider the massive impact this scheme had upon my professional development and the vast number of teaching ideas I developed through contact with a close network of colleagues.

In Chapter 8 I look at the complexities and the enormous potential value of working with teaching assistants (TAs). In my current role I have had the great pleasure of working with very many TAs, both in schools and through continuing professional development courses I have provided for TAs, working in both primary and secondary schools. I explore typical issues related to some of the work they do in mathematics classrooms, basing some of my writing on comments offered to me. Hearing some of their stories related to the many different ways their talents are utilized in classrooms creates a rich tapestry.

Chapter 9 focuses upon the notion of 'progression' in pupils' learning of mathematics. My starting point is based upon my belief that learning mathematics does not occur in a linear way, nor is it conceived at the same rate or depth. This leads me to discuss the issue of interconnectedness; to consider ways in which we can cause pupils to make connections between the different concepts they learn in mathematics. I also explore the link between progression and differentiated learning. Again in this chapter I suggest ideas for the classroom, each of which has been well tested.

Chapter 10 is about resources. What I have sought to offer in this chapter is a wide range of grids and manipulatives that I have used in almost forty years of teaching. By 'eck, writing that sentence stopped me in my tracks . . . have I really been teaching that long?

Making the first tentative steps into a mathematics classroom

Being a 'newcomer' and doing anything for the first time, whether as a youngster or as an adult, brings with it anticipation and expectation, apprehension and possibly trepidation. As we make our first tentative steps into a new project or into a new arena we may gain a sense of exhilaration, while at the same time finding complexities and challenges; emotions often abound as we meet these challenges. The business of learning is certainly emotive and, as a teacher, it is useful to recognize the impact the emotional, or affective, domain of learning has upon cognitive aspects of learning. I develop this issue of affective and cognitive learning further in Chapter 9.

Can you remember for example when you first attempted to ride a bike or when you first tried to learn to swim? Perhaps when you were a little older you might have tried orienteering or hung on for dear life on your first climbing escapade! Can you remember the awkwardness and the pleasure at saying your first stuttering sentence in another language, perhaps while on a holiday in France or Spain? As a youngster I remember the absolute pleasure of finding myself riding my bicycle without my best friend holding onto the saddle and running beside me. I can even remember where the event took place on Albion Street in Burnley. As a teenager I remember my first trip to Anfield in the early 1960s for an FA cup replay between Liverpool and Burnley. I even remember Ronnie Moran scoring a late winner from a penalty and the local policeman celebrating with the fans in the Kop, the feeling of being overwhelmed by the passion, the noise and the excitement (a feeling I still get). As adults we engage in new or different experiences or events such as going for a job interview or visiting another country for the first time. Going solo for the first time in a classroom, however, must rate as one of the most dauntingly scary and potentially uplifting experiences I can ever remember.

By the time you go solo you will have had a range of opportunities and classroom experiences to prepare yourself for this first independent bash at teaching. For example, you will, hopefully, have already met the class and know something about some of the pupils. You may have worked with small groups so some kind of relationship will have begun to be formed. Nothing, however, can fully prepare you for that first solo experience of teaching a whole class for a whole lesson, an event that may feel to stretch to eternity while having the potential for being over in a flash.

Planning your first lesson

You are likely to have been given a lot of advice about teaching, some of it possibly contradictory. Some will be fundamentally important, while other advice may be glib and not necessarily supportive. Planning lessons in order to become confident about the main 'stages' or planned inputs is clearly a vital part of the process; it is how to plan and what to plan for that is important. As a minimum and at a macro level, I believe we need to plan for:

- a 'rich' starting-point question or task for pupils to work on/explore
- some extension tasks
- the resources you will need
- the strategies you might employ.

The planning needs to be underpinned by certain key knowledge, such as where any lesson fits into a scheme of work and roughly what prior experiences of the content knowledge you are planning to teach pupils in the class (in the main) will have previously met. Thus you will need to know what content knowledge you are aiming your planning at. With all of this in mind I offer a pro forma that will, I expect, be different to the kind of templates you may have met in your training. It is based upon a minimalist approach in order to maximize your planning-for-teaching time. As an example I have chosen to focus on planning to teach decimals. However, any concept could be inserted in the place of 'decimal' or 'decimals'. The fundamental idea is to invite you to be explicit about your knowledge and understanding of what underpins decimals and, therefore, to encourage you to consider what activities to plan.

What does decimal mean?

Why do we need decimals?

Write two contexts where pupils are likely to meet decimals.

What other concepts are closely linked to decimals?

What knowledge as an absolute minimum would any child need to have in order to begin to understand decimals?

You are invited to spend a few minutes completing the pro forma before reading on.

One outcome of being explicit about what you think 'decimal' means is that you can start from your own conception, rather than that of a textbook or a published scheme. This is important because all too often there exists uncritical belief in what the textbook has to offer and unless you have worked through each question from an exercise, you are exposing yourself to a situation where a pupil might actually find an error within the text that, in turn, could lead to a misconception being formed. Should this occur you may either unwittingly compound a pupil's misconception or you will have to unpick the mistake. Either way, the time would be better spent by thinking through the basics of the concept yourself. The second question, about why we need decimals, is to encourage you to be crystal clear about what underpins the concept of decimals; that without them we would only be able to operate either with whole numbers or with fractional amounts. The third question about 'real' contexts is equally important. We need to be careful about whether contexts are truly real or whether they are pseudo real. If you have decided the former, then you need to ensure that they are truly real to the pupils and not an adult context in which the pupils may have little interest. If you decide upon the latter, then you may need to be circumspect about using such contexts as a convenience to justify teaching something. If you are convinced as to the truly real value of a context, then use this context within your planning. If, on the other hand, you cannot find any truly real context, then you may wish to adopt a 'pure' mathematical approach and plan for some kind of problem-solving task. Here the context itself becomes that of problem solving. In the introduction I suggested a task intended to be viewed as a problem-solving approach for students to work with the decimal notation, based upon a place value grid that includes the tenths column.

Starting and surviving a first full lesson

To plan and teach your first full, solo lesson, the main objectives, I would imagine, are to survive relatively unscathed and to have gained a sense that it was a good experience. There are all kinds of questions you may need to think about and plan for when you are going to teach your first lesson, such as:

- How will I survive the lesson?
- What might I say at the beginning?
- Where might my attention be when the pupils are walking into the room?
- What will I do if I can't get them quiet at the beginning?
- How will I keep control?
- How will I keep the class on task?

The answers to these questions will, to a large degree, depend upon the kind of expectations pupils have about what being in a mathematics classroom is usually all about. I develop this issue of classroom culture in the next chapter. For now, two examples of culture that are likely to pertain more to a secondary context might be whether students are a) expected to line up outside the door waiting for the class teacher to let them in and b) once in the room whether they are expected to stand behind their chairs. At the other end of this waiting-for-a-lesson-to-begin spectrum, students might be used to coming directly into the classroom and sitting at their desks. Clearly there is an issue of 'when in Rome', which may need to be initially played out, particularly for a trainee or a NQT.

Thinking through these beginning-of-lesson events at a micro level may involve thinking about what else you might do as the class is entering the room. Where might you stand? Will you choose to make eye contact with some of the students as they enter the room? Will you choose to greet the students in some way or another? What aspects of the students' behaviour as they enter the classroom might you insist upon and what might you choose to ignore? These are questions you may wish to contemplate and rehearse. Of course, what happens in reality will depend upon all kinds of actions and outcomes that cannot be anticipated and which, in the light of experience, makes teaching such a fantastic job. The more we learn to live with the unexpected, and find our inner teaching skills and talents to learn to deal with unanticipated outcomes, is essential. 'Expect the unexpected' may be something of a catchphrase, but it is one that certainly pertains to a teacher's engagement in some of the many social interactions that take place over the course of a lesson. You may wish to read an article on the Association of Teachers of Mathematics website from *Mathematics Teaching,* MT153, entitled 'An unexpected dream' (1995).

Putting on an act or being your natural self

All too often trainee teachers feel they need to put on some kind of 'performance'. The difficulty with this notion is that the focus becomes one of the teacher as a performer rather than the teacher as a facilitator of learning. This may be because the trainee is being observed and feels expected to put on some kind of performance. I have seen so many lessons where the trainee has 'worked too hard' and the pupils were either sitting back or were passengers journeying on the trainee's lesson plan. The important issue is about finding the balance between who does the work. Teachers cannot do the learning for the pupils and cannot assume they can make pupils understand something (I develop this issue of balance in Chapter 5). Pupils clearly have a responsibility for what they learn and this aspect of learning needs to be worked on, discussed and clarified from lesson one onwards.

Being one's 'natural' self, however, as opposed to being an actor on the stage, is something I believe worthy of consideration. All too often teaching is thought of or described as 'putting on an act'. The problem arises, however, if the act is not particularly good or 'entertaining' or if the act cannot be sustained. Pupils are expert at recognizing falsehoods and facades. Of course, we need to participate in and hopefully enjoy the interactions, the cut and the thrust, and the 'drama' of the classroom. If we didn't, there would be something missing. We need at times to be 'larger than life' yet on such occasions it is important that pupils recognize this is one part of the teacher's style. This is different to being somebody who you are not.

To avoid the need to put on an act, it is worth contemplating how to get a class started on a task as quickly as possible, thus negating the possibility of turning the front of the classroom into a stage. One way to try to achieve this is to offer a class a seemingly simple problem to work on that has potential for differentiated developments and outcomes. Offering something that is easy to set up, demonstrate and explain (or even better to invite some pupils to take part in the initial demonstration and explanation) feels to be an important criterion. Getting a class working on a task as quickly as possible, therefore, with minimal teacher input means the focus of attention shifts away from the teacher having to 'teach' to the pupils having to engage with a task, so the focus is upon learning.

An easy-to-offer idea, say for a Year 6 or a Year 7 class, might be the 'diagonal through a rectangle' problem (see *Points of Departure 1*, idea 57, an excellent publication by the ATM, containing many valuable ideas).

The problem goes as follows:

- Draw a rectangle on 1cm- or even better 2cm-squared paper.
- Draw a diagonal line from the bottom left through to the top right-hand corner.
- Record the number of squares the diagonal passes through, for example in a 6 by 3 rectangle the diagonal passes through six squares.

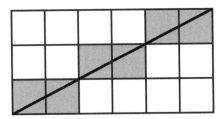

The task now is to draw more rectangles and to find how many squares the diagonal passes through. The idea is to try to find a way of predicting the number of squares passed through as a function of the dimensions of the rectangle. The beauty of this idea is the ease involved in setting it up and how it does not require a great deal of teacher instruction.

Using an idea such as 'diagonal through a rectangle' has many useful attributes and fulfils a range of planning criteria:

- The problem is an excellent way of getting a class speedily started on a task.
- The problem is easy for pupils to collect information, yet provides mathematical challenges for pupils to seek connections between the dimensions of a rectangle and the number of squares passed through by the diagonal.
- The problem is supportive of creative, problem-solving approaches to teaching and learning.
- The problem has inbuilt opportunities for differentiated learning so the idea can be developed and extended.
- The problem can be used with a class containing pupils of a wide range of potential attainments (for example, a mixed-ability class).
- By working on the problem, pupils can integrate the 'using and applying' with the 'number and algebra' attainment target 2. Thus, the 'diagonals' problem encourages systematic working, conjecturing and generalizing. With regard to Ma2, pupils will be working on divisors and highest common multiples.
- The problem provides inbuilt opportunities for the teacher to assess the way some pupils organize themselves.
- The problem might be initially worked on individually; later pairs or small groups of pupils could pool their results.

All in all, therefore, this simple-to-explain task engages with a range of lesson planning objectives and yet does not require very much preparation. However, this leads to a centrally important issue about a trainee teacher's readiness to teach and the key preparations that may be required.

Planning for teaching

Perhaps the most important aspect of planning for teaching is for the trainee or the new teacher to be confident about working through a task in order to become confident with the idea, such as the 'diagonals' problem. Gaining a clear sense of where the task leads and the kind of questions you might pose to pupils who either become 'stuck' or who will benefit from having their thinking extended is a key aspect of planning. Playing around with ideas is an important aspect of gaining confidence in a task. This aspect of the planning process is a far more valuable use of your time than filling in copious amounts of information on someone else's, usually a standardized college or school's, lesson-planning pro forma.

As such, I strongly encourage all trainees, mathematics teachers and NQTs to purchase either the four *Points of Departure* publications (PoD 1, 2, 3, 4) costing approximately £20 from the ATM (www.atm.org.uk) or, for primary trainees, the compilation *Primary Points of Departure*. I can guarantee it will be the best £20 you will ever spend. Buy them for yourselves and don't leave them for colleagues to walk off with; have them as your bedside reading and get to know them inside out – they are fantastic!

Below are two ideas from each of the four publications that fit the same planning criteria as described above:

1. palindromes – PoD 1, idea 34 (see below)
2. discs – PoD 1, idea 12 (see Chapter 8)
3. number cells – PoD 2, idea 3 (see below)
4. dotty shapes – PoD 2, idea 26
5. skewed Pascal – PoD 3, idea 10
6. 10 × 12 or 11 × 11? – PoD 3, idea 24
7. connect four – PoD 4, idea 22
8. sticky triangles – PoD 4, idea 39

I have developed two of these ideas, 'palindromic numbers' and 'number cells' in order to reaffirm just how far a simple idea can be developed. The following is an extract from *100+ Ideas for Teaching Mathematics* (Ollerton: 2007):

Choose a two-digit number and write it down, for example:	39
Reverse it	93
Add	132 (stage 1)
Reverse it	231
Add	363 (stage 2)
Stop here because the answer, 363, is palindromic.	

39 can now be classified as a two-stage number.

How many stages do other numbers take?

Challenges such as finding four-stage and six-stage numbers will provide a class with plenty to work on.

If different stages are colour coded, students might make use of a 100 square and colour in every number according to how many stages each takes. There will, of course, be several zero-stage numbers that are already palindromic, such as 11, 22, 33, and so on.

Students might be encouraged to explore why palindromic answers produced in this way all are multiples of 11. Trying to explain why this is the case would provide some students with a worthy challenge.

A harder problem is to consider palindromic multiplication when two two-digit numbers are used, for example 96 × 23 = 32 × 69.

In terms of planning, to use this particular idea I must forewarn you that starting with 89 (or 98 obviously), requires a lengthy list of calculations. All I will offer at this point is that there is a solution that after 24 stages works out to 8,813,200,023,188 so at least I have saved you having to do a bit of arithmetic!

The palindromic multiplication task will provide students with much to contemplate. Using the well known 'grid method' for multiplication in order to see how all the component parts fit together when calculating 96 × 23 followed by 32 × 69 may enable students to analyse what happens and why the puzzle works the way it does.

Like palindromic numbers, the next idea, number cells, only requires simple addition in the first instance, yet there is potential for developing the task into writing formulae. Start with any two numbers as the first two values of a cell of five numbers, for example 4 and 5. Now find the next three numbers by performing a Fibonacci-type calculation, that is 4 + 5 = 9, 5 + 9 = 14.

4	5	9	14	23

The idea now is to provide students with the first and last values and they have to calculate the missing three middle numbers.

Once they have worked out some teacher-set tasks they need to make up their own number cell problems and ask someone else to work out their missing numbers. Students can be encouraged to begin with a higher first number than second number and they can try working with negative values or fractional amounts; there is plenty of scope. A further challenge is to calculate the five values before the first one; here there will be an excellent opportunity to work with negative numbers and some students might be able to derive 'rules' for 'subtracting a negative'. There is plenty up for grabs even at this non-algebraic stage.

Students can engage with algebra by setting up the following question: 'If we know the first value (f) and the last value (l) in a five-cell configuration, how can the middle cell (m) be determined?'

Students will need to gather some data here in order to recognize that m is one third of the sum of f and l or $m = 1/3(f + l)$. Seeing how m relates to f and l for other odd amounts of number cells produces a most interesting result.

What pupils need to get good at is to learn how to collect information and stick with a problem, how to develop a problem, how to work independently (for example, without a textbook), how to explore an idea, how to look for patterns, how to look for generality and how to conjecture. Learning how to work in such ways ('stickability', developmentally, independently, seeking pattern, generalizing and conjecturing) is 100 per cent connected to pupils' views of what it means to 'do' mathematics. This, in turn, is determined by the classroom culture, which I develop further in the next chapter.

Learning these processes as well as such personal skills is something that needs to happen from an early age and in my limited experience occurs frequently in KS1 classrooms. However, for a trainee or a relatively new teacher in a school, seeking to enculturate pupils into valuing problem solving and working in ways described above might be seen as problematic, particularly if the pupils are not expected to or are not used to working with more open problems, or whose experience of 'doing' mathematics has been largely by responding to questions from worksheets or textbook exercises. Any teacher, however experienced they are, needs to recognize the predominant culture in which learning and teaching currently takes place and, if they wish to make changes to the way pupils engage with mathematics, needs to recognize that small steps are important. However, I recognize myself as an impatient beast and that trying to stick to such advice is not always easy.

An issue for consideration in this chapter is about one's sphere of influence. For a trainee or an NQT this will be inevitably limited, yet will exist to some degree. Widening one's sphere of influence is about developing one's teaching style, becoming explicit about one's emerging pedagogy and broadening the range of ideas we take with us into classrooms. The more ideas we have to take into classrooms, the more scope we have for developing our confidence... now there's a word.

Classroom culture

What kind of learning culture do you want to have in your mathematics classroom? How do you want your classroom to look, sound and feel?

In this chapter I shall attempt to work on answers to these questions from my perspective, while recognizing there are all manner of issues beyond the classroom that impact upon pupils' lives and, therefore, guide what happens in any classroom, some of which can 'stretch' the gifts of any teacher.

The learning culture in any classroom is determined, in part, by the ethos that pervades the school as a whole. I shall consider issues of classroom culture and make reference to the kind of tasks, puzzles and problems I believe support the development of a positive learning culture. First of all, however, I feel it is important to look at the kind of impact that whole-school ethos has upon individual classroom culture.

A comprehensive school I had the pleasure to teach in was frequently described by visitors as having a pleasant and welcoming atmosphere. So often was this type of comment made I eventually started asking people to try to define exactly what it was about the school that caused them to make such observations. Of course, answers were rarely easily come by and responses often involved lots of hand waving and offerings such as, 'Well you know ...' The phrase 'squeezing jelly' comes to mind. Seeking to define what creates a conducive, supportive, welcoming atmosphere is not easy. Visitors were clearly picking up on all kinds of signs, stimuli and behaviours. It would be disingenuous, however, to suggest that everything was sweetness and light; there were difficult times and some students faced significant challenges both inside and outside the school. Nevertheless, for most of the time the school operated on a basis of positive interactions between staff and students and between staff and staff. I am sure what I have described here will be recognized by many people.

I have also been in schools where I have sensed antagonism and antipathy. I am aware, therefore, of the impact school ethos has upon the classroom cultures that individual teachers seek to create. In order to support individual teachers to create a sound, effective culture of learning in their classrooms, we must recognize the impact that whole-school ethos has upon such an aim.

School ethos, democracy, signs and symbols

School ethos begins at the 'top' and filters its way through every fibre of the life of a school. Teachers at the 'chalkface' are supported by strategic, clearly thought-out rationale. Just what the teachers in any school want the ethos to be will depend upon whether they have any opportunity to help determine or construct it in the first instance. When teachers feel empowered by democratic decision making they can, in turn, seek to empower their students. The following quote from Shor (1992: 11) offers an interesting challenge: 'A school year that begins by questioning school could be a remarkably democratic learning experience for the students.' Democracy, now there's an interesting concept!

There are large signs and symbols and there are small ones. An example of a seemingly small sign might be whether the headteacher has a marked parking space, usually close to the entrance. Another example is whether photographs of the staff in the reception area are arranged in alphabetic order or in a way that defines the pyramid/power structure in a school. There is a highly successful comprehensive school in the Midlands, according to inspection reports, which I have visited many times, which operates a mixed-ability structure (large sign). In the reception area there are photographs of every Year 9 student, each one wearing something, or holding an artefact, which signifies their best subject. Any visitor to the school could not fail to see this and in some way be captivated by the display of achievement and students' interests.

A further example of a set of 'large' signs, or principles, which were all bundled together in a school in Derbyshire I visited were:

- mixed ability throughout
- no school uniform
- no end of lesson bells
- staff and students referred to each other on first name terms.

This may sound like some teachers' version of anarchy, their worst nightmare. The reality, however, was an atmosphere of feeling welcomed and staff who seemed clearly at ease with the ethos that underpinned the school. That the school taught in mixed-ability tutor groups meant the ethos was one of equality and a positive intention not to label students according to the notion of 'setting by ability'. The absence of school uniform created an ethos of respect for individuals to make decisions about their dress code. There were only two bells each day (first thing in the morning and after lunch). There were no end of lesson bells; here the ethos is one that puts teachers in control of exactly when their lesson finishes. Students were not 'waiting for the bell' so, within a couple of minutes either way, teachers have a degree of autonomy about when a lesson ends. The issue of staff and students being on first name terms is another interesting way of people working together and supports a tradition of mutual and equal respect.

Whole-school ethos is something senior staff have significant responsibility to help create in their school. How this is achieved and how all staff are provided with opportunities to participate in decision making and development of ethos is fundamentally important. The more responsibility ceded to staff, the more they can replicate this process in their classrooms and the more they are enabled to recognize how the classroom culture they wish to create is supported by the ethos in the school.

Learning culture

To begin this section I invite you to consider what kind of learning culture you would like to help create in your classroom. This is a bit like asking you for your three wishes, though I am unable to act as the 'good fairy' and grant them. I think it is useful, however, to list ways you would like your students to learn mathematics in your classroom. Perhaps you might like to write a short list and compare it with mine. I have put six items on my list:

- Students learn how to ask questions about a task or problem.
- Students want to develop a task because they are interested in doing so.
- Students make choices about how best to work on a task.

- Students learn to look for and bring previously learned mathematics to the solution of a new problem.
- Students develop a sense of the power of mathematics.
- Students see value in learning mathematics.

Students learn how to ask questions about a task or problem

To foster a questioning culture it is important to make sure students know this is valued and, therefore, must be explicitly encouraged. One way I have developed this approach has been to set up a situation and then asked students, perhaps working in pairs, to generate some questions they could ask about the situation or about the resource. An example of this approach is to offer a problem such as the one below.

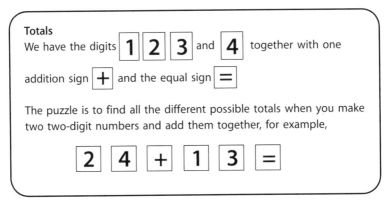

The value of using this task is the ease with which it can be posed yet it has interesting depths that, conceptually, are about place value and ordering. Having set this problem I can invite students to consider what kind of questions they might ask of this situation. Of course, causing students to ask questions is, in itself, a learned skill. By getting them to work in a pair or in a group of three, for no more than 2 or 3 minutes, and in that time to create some questions they might ask about this situation is one strategy. If I have used such a strategy on many previous occasions, then they will get used to recognizing that this is all part of what learning mathematics is all about; I am enculturing a questioning approach to their learning.

Typical questions to emerge from experienced questioners are:

- How many different totals are there?
- What is the largest total?
- What is the smallest total?
- Can I prove I have found them all?
- Are there any patterns in the totals?
- Can we use different numbers?
- What happens if we multiply instead of adding?

Mathematically, I want students to try to find all the different totals, to try to prove they have found them all and ultimately seek to generalize for maximum and minimum totals (and/or products) by considering what the arrangements are for values a, b, c, d where $a < b < c < d$. What is also useful about this problem is to cause students to see that when two-digit numbers are formed (ab) this is actually $10a + 1b$ and as I stated above, this is where place value needs to be considered.

Students want to develop a task because they are interested in doing so

'We cannot force anyone to be interested in anything.' Most parents will recognize the truth about this statement in relation to their children. We can, however, try to create a climate that, at best, will not be boring for students. Interest, in part, is about making the learning of mathematics achievable and in part about what we give value to. If value is usually given to the first person to answer a question or to the person who completes an exercise or a worksheet, then this is what students will come to value and see as being important. If, however, we give value to 'good' questions, to interesting answers, to effort and to stickability, then these are the kinds of qualities students, in the main, will want to exhibit. Seeking to create a culture based upon interest must beget tasks and problems to which the student can become interested in finding a solution.

At one ATM Easter conference, I attended this issue of enculturation and interest and how long it takes to create such a culture was brought home to me in a quite stunning way in a session led by Anne Watson. In the session, mathematical 'surprises' were high on Anne's agenda and the level of interest she created was palpable. Here is one example of a task Anne offered. All she did was to give out a slip of paper with the information shown and invited delegates to fill in the blanks.

0	0	1	0
1 6	0.5		
1 3		0.5	
1 2	1	0	
2 3			
5 6	0.5	−0.5	
1	0	−1	

In ATM tradition, I am not going to provide any answers, though anybody who reads this will have met such information in their own mathematical education.

Within 20 or so minutes, having been given problems that held surprises, we were convinced there was always going to be something deeper to look for than necessarily existed. Thus, when Anne offered delegates one problem where there was no surprise lurking, just about everyone in the room looked for 'the catch' or the surprise and as a consequence viewed a straightforward problem with degrees of what might be described as 'healthy' suspicion. This adult audience had, therefore, been enculturated into a view of mathematics based upon careful scrutiny of the information and being wary of suggesting the obvious.

Clearly the issue of developing a classroom culture that combines all kinds of ways of working on tasks and problems is important. Of greater importance, however, was how mathematical structures, which everyone already knew about, could still be made interesting and intriguing in the way tasks were presented.

Students make choices about how best to work on a task

One of the more difficult aspects of creating a culture of choice is what the teacher might do should some student make an inappropriate choice; how long the teacher decides to let the student continue in a seemingly unprofitable direction before deciding to intervene is an interesting tension. Offering students choice is inevitably going to be a risky business, yet how are youngsters going to learn anything if all they ever do is to follow the teacher's methods and algorithms and produce answers to closed questions?

One aspect of choice is about providing students with more open questions to work on for which there is either more than one way of tackling the problem or more than one answer to be found. An example is a problem based upon making compound shapes with rectangles. The idea begins with two congruent rectangles drawn on 1cm-squared paper. The first task is to fold each rectangle in half, one along a vertical line of symmetry and the other along its horizontal line of symmetry, as in the diagram below.

Once each rectangle has been folded in half and, if the dimensions of the original rectangle were, say, 6cm by 10cm, then the dimensions of the folded-in-half shapes will clearly be 3cm by 10cm and 6cm by 5cm.

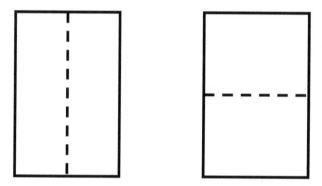

Using these two rectangles students can a) count around the perimeter (P) of each rectangle and b) find area (A) of each rectangle. The purpose of doing this, beyond it being a counting task, is for students to recognize that concepts of perimeter and area are 'generally' not connected. This is because we are working in different units of measure; while one can create a formula to connect P and A for regular polygons, this is as far as it goes, as in the main P and A are not connected. So for these two shapes, while the area is constant ($30cm^2$) their perimeters are different (26cm and 22cm respectively).

The main part of the task is for students to produce compound shapes by joining one of each rectangle together and seeing what different perimeters of shapes can be made. For example, the perimeter of the shape below, counting around anticlockwise from the bottom left-hand corner, is the sum of $10 + 3 + (10 - 5) + 6 + 5 + 6 + 3$, or 38cm.

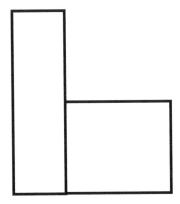

In this problem students have choices about the different compound shapes they make. They also have choice about how to calculate the different perimeters, that is they can either count the distance all around the actual perimeter of the shape or they can subtract twice the common, joined edge lengths and subtract this from the total of the perimeters of the two separate rectangles.

Proving all the different possible perimeters have been found will provide one challenge. A further challenge would be to express the different perimeters algebraically by labelling the original rectangle as **w** (width) and **l** (length). This task could be developed by considering the perimeters of compound shapes made from two of one piece and one of the other and so on.

A particularly creative, alternative solution was presented to me when I had offered this task to a group of teachers from a department. This was to overlap the shapes as in the diagram below. Not only can we consider perimeter, we can also see how the area changes.

The issue of making choices here is an interesting one. If I were to suggest to a student that this solution does not fit 'my rules', then I am not really offering choice. I might think this new rule is going to take the student up a blind alley and, therefore, want to prevent the student from wasting their time. However, such a suggestion might also lead to a rich vein of further investigation ... and I might also be wrong.

Students learn to look for and bring previously learned mathematics to the solution of a new problem

This is by no means straightforward. Students do not explicitly think, 'What do I know that might help me solve this problem?' Neither do they necessarily know what mathematical tools (concepts) they have in their toolkit that they might use. The issues here are about:

- Helping students become explicit about the mathematics they have learned.
- Enabling students to become fluent with the use of mathematics in situations they meet that transcend the immediacy of their initial exposure to specific concepts.

These approaches to teaching are at the other end to objectives stated at the beginning of a lesson, about which I have significant concerns. I am far more interested in students knowing what they have learned than for me to tell them what I intend them to learn. This is partly because in every classroom there will be as many differentiated levels of understanding as there are students. Asking students, therefore, to explicitly consider, at the end of a module of work, what they feel they have achieved, what they have understood and how any of this is connected to previous learning is useful.

How students are encouraged to become explicit about their learning is another interesting cultural issue. For example, if students come to expect that 'writing' about mathematics is a normal aspect of learning mathematics then we can use this to good effect. Of course writing for some students will be harder than doing the mathematics itself, so it is important to offer students different ways of recording what they think they have learned. Making notes, using diagrams, creating both large and mini posters or doing a full write up are all ways of enabling explicitness. So for example, taking the '1234 + =' problem described previously, students could make a poster to demonstrate how they have worked on the problem and explain any findings they have produced. Causing students to create maps of their learning is also useful and I develop this further in Chapter 9.

Students develop a sense of the power of mathematics

Students are more likely to develop a sense of the power of mathematics if their teacher genuinely and explicitly see such power in mathematics themself. I am not suggesting here that teachers needs to demonstrate 'anorak' tendencies towards mathematics, though I guess we want to enjoy our interactions with students and this, in part, might be to show what value we place in the discipline. Discipline is a useful word for describing mathematics; to become evermore skilled in its uses and applications, students need to practise the art of mental imagery. This is because mathematics, first and foremost, is a discipline of the mind. While learners need to use concrete manipulatives to record their mathematical thinking, the initial thought processes involved are abstract. Number, for example, is a generalized understanding of an amount; the same number can represent an amount of physical objects, perhaps arranged in different ways, a measure of time, of distance, of weight, of area, of money, of volume, a score, an answer to a calculation. In our mind's eye we need to accommodate the different ways numbers are represented and the different contexts in which numbers appear; we need to achieve fluency in operating with numbers.

The power of mathematics lies in seeing how these representations can be manipulated, dissected and put back together, how they can be increased and decreased, how they operate within the place value system, within the coordinate system, take on different forms, for example standard index form, as a product of prime factors. As such we need to help students appreciate that learning different representations, specific vocabulary and being able to switch their understanding from one context to another are significant achievements; we take this for granted at their peril. I could create similar lists for algebra and geometry.

The power of learning mathematics, therefore, lies in students demonstrating their capability to manipulate numbers, symbols, formulae and properties; of being able to see when one representation is more useful or more appropriate than another. This is connected to the choices students make about the problems they are given to work on, as well as the fluency they display in using a particular skill or process. An example of choice and fluency might be seen as students work on a problem such as 'How many different triangles are there in a square 16-

dot grid?' A precursor to this problem might be an exploration of the different triangles there are on a square 9-dot grid, so with the 16-dot grid the idea would be to look for new triangles.

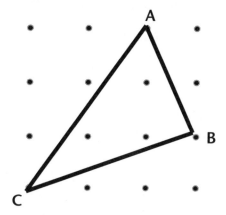

In the example above the three lengths are AB = $\sqrt{5}$, BC = $\sqrt{10}$ and AC = $\sqrt{13}$. The choice students might make could be about the order they decide to use to make the different triangles and how they go about ordering their collection. So, for example they might decide to fix two points and consider the possible position of the third point. In terms of fluency, this might focus students' attention on using surds or perhaps using a vector description. At issue here is whether they are encouraged to draw upon their own toolboxes of mathematics or whether the teacher suggests an approach of fixing two points, of using surds or vectors as ways of describing their collection. This problem could be developed to calculate the different possible angles in each triangle and this, in turn, would draw upon students' ability to use their trigonometric knowledge. Clearly the more decisions students make, the more they are going to think and work and engage with and 'feel' the power of mathematics.

Students see value in learning mathematics

I think the most debilitating question a teacher has to face is: 'Why are we learning all this stuff?' The problem for the teacher is threefold. First, the teacher is unlikely to be able to offer a rational explanation because the student is unlikely to be sufficiently interested in the answer. Second, the question may have been asked because the student is an expert teacher-baiter and knows this is 'the' question that will wind Sir/Miss up. Third, because this may not really be the question they wanted to ask. It may have been 'Why am I so bored?' Of course, it might be a perfectly honest, analytical question and, if this were the case, then it could be a question worthy of praise; in the main, however, this explanation might be somewhat unlikely. I am not going to insult you by trying to offer a 'useful' riposte because everything depends upon context and the general relationship that exists between teacher and student. Asking students what they think the point of learning mathematics is (before the question is asked) might, however, be a useful way of creating an honest and open dialogue about 'why learn mathematics'.

I believe there are two important reasons for learning mathematics. The first relates to a 'pure', problem-solving view of the world, about seeing how abstract concepts connect together and the development of skills of systematization, generality, conjecture and proof. I call this 'functioning mathematically'. The second reason for learning mathematics is because it is used and applied in all kinds of social and economic contexts and I think of this as 'functional mathematics'. The notion of 'real-life mathematics', however, is contestable. What is real to an adult, an employer, an examination question writer or certainly a mathematics textbook author is not always (or ever) the same as what is real to adolescents or pre-adolescents. Students' concerns are rarely about finding the cost of VAT on an article or working out how much it would cost to decorate their bedroom. In many ways these are pseudo contexts and at worst 'con-texts'. The complexity for the mathematics teacher is looking for authentic ways that are likely to motivate students, thus causing them to engage with mathematics.

While looking for situations that are real to students it is also important to utilize those that transcend the immediacy of students' lives; this is so students are able to recognize the purpose mathematics serves both inside and outside their own life contexts.

Such functional aspects of learning mathematics can be ascribed to notions of modelling; using mathematics to model and make sense of real-life situations is a key feature of problem-solving aspects of learning mathematics.

How any teacher is able to motivate their students to learn mathematics through functional, real-life contexts would seem to be dependent upon a teacher's:

- relationship with a class
- confidence to use real-life stimuli in their teaching
- access to materials/stimuli that they might choose to use/adapt for their students or that would be appropriate to the local environment
- utilization of contexts that are within and beyond students' immediate lives
- awareness of what mathematics they want students to gain from a particular stimulus.

Differences between classroom culture and classroom atmosphere

I conclude this chapter with a brief discussion about the difference between culture and atmosphere. Determining what classroom atmosphere any teacher wishes to have in their classroom is not easy. There are so many different factors that impact upon classroom atmosphere it is difficult to know where to start in order to capture a workable definition. What is 100 per cent certain, however, is that all teachers' classrooms have an atmosphere and students will have weighed up, or are in the process of weighing up, what it means to walk into a mathematics lesson with Ms P, an English lesson with Mr Q or a D&T lesson with Mrs R.

To close this chapter and in order to draw a final comparison between atmosphere and culture I use the issue of 'expectations' and apply it to:

- classroom atmosphere
- the culture of working mathematically.

Classroom atmosphere

Students will know something of each teacher's expectations and about the stated or unstated 'rules' that they are intended to conform to within each classroom. Indeed, sussing out a teacher's expectations is probably the first thing students do, either consciously or subconsciously. They become aware of how the teacher walks, talks, gesticulates, stands, crouches down and what implicit messages this range of body language gives out. The teacher, meanwhile, may become evermore conscious of the impact of their body language and the expectations she or he intends to convey at different times in a lesson. Of course, all these implicit messages and expectations are being transmitted while other things are happening, that is when the teacher is in the action of teaching, waiting for a class to settle, or talking to the whole class, to a small group or to an individual. Messages are conveyed when the teacher is not talking to anyone and is perhaps sitting or standing at the back of the room, or even when not in the room. This last point may sound like the beginnings of anarchy and sedition. However, many teachers know when they can trust a class by not being there in the room. This is in contrast to always needing to be there to maintain order. Indeed, one key measure of a teacher's expectations is what happens when a class can be trusted to get on with their work without needing constant supervision.

The culture of working mathematically

In summary, teaching and learning mathematics is:

- essentially about pattern spotting and seeking generality.
- using problem-solving approaches for teaching and learning mathematics.
- developing a 'have a go' culture in students.
- asking questions such as: 'Have you found all the possible solutions?' 'How do you know?' or 'Can you explain how you know?'
- living without a textbook or repetitive worksheet; practise and consolidation activity emerging from problems that we offer students.
- enabling mathematics to emerge through kinesthetic approaches so students can touch and see mathematics first hand as well as relying upon teachers' explanations or a visual demonstration via an interactive whiteboard.
- going 'back to basics', helping students understand and be able to return to first principles.
- teaching in an 'interconnected' way, so skills are not taught in isolation.
- developing students' mathematics through in-depth approaches rather than skimming over concepts.
- engaging students in the 'beauty' of mathematics and encouraging creativity.

The teacher's role in helping develop such a culture becomes more about making strategic interventions and asking questions based upon what students are doing, rather than always giving detailed explanations about how to do something.

What we believe is what we teach

We teach what we believe but do we believe what we teach? In this chapter, I invite you to reflect upon some of the ways you were taught mathematics. What were the high points and the low points? Can you remember a time when you found mathematics interesting? Can you remember a time when you were bored out of your mind? Can you remember being challenged to think hard in mathematics lessons or do you remember the textbooks and doing endless exercises? Perhaps you had a relatively neutral experience of mathematics, though I wonder if this would be the case for the majority of people.

My conjecture is that returning to one's roots, however joyful or painful, confirmatory or contradictory, can be useful in order to try to make sense of the ways we currently teach mathematics. One of the difficulties for us as teachers in trying to make sense of what constitutes effective teaching is that, in the main, we are the 'successes' of a system of school mathematics that 'failed' many of our peers. Predominantly, I continue to conjecture, we will have experienced mostly 'top set', drill and skill type experiences as learners of mathematics that (may have) 'worked' for us. However, it is very difficult to know how our peers, for whom mathematics was largely about failure and pointlessness, received their mathematics education. By making such a journey back to past events, therefore, we can attempt to stand in our current pupils' shoes, to see how learning mathematics might currently appear to them; we can try to get closer to what our pupils feel and what might be the 'highs' and the 'lows' for them when they are learning mathematics.

Reflecting in this way may provide us with insights; a rationale for teaching the way we teach. Retelling and analysing anecdotes is intended to act as a vehicle for confirming or challenging one's approaches to teaching mathematics. If the latter comes to the fore and emerges as an issue for us to work on, this may, potentially, create a desire to develop and to change some of the ways we teach.

As examples I have two anecdotes about my schooling; one is about learning mathematics and the other is about sitting the eleven-plus. The first goes back to when I was a pupil at Rosehill Primary School in Burnley in the late 1950s, when Bill Hayley and the Comets were rocking round the clock, and Wolverhampton Wanderers were the team to beat in the Football League Division One.

The first anecdote refers to subtraction. As an example I refer to the following calculation: 953 – 687. The method I was taught was described as 'borrow from the top and pay back on the doorstep' and I would have written the following in my exercise book:

$$
\begin{array}{ccc}
\text{H} & \text{T} & \text{U} \\
9 & {}^15 & {}^13 \\
-{}_16 & {}_18 & 7 \\
\hline
2 & 6 & 6
\end{array}
$$

Try picking the bones out of that!

Not got it yet? Well, here is how the method worked.

Starting with the units column we were taught to say:

Step 1:   '*7 from 3 you cannot do*' (mathematically this is a completely untrue statement – but I deal with that later).

Step 2:   '*Borrow one* (1) *from the top...*' (this meant borrowing one ten from the T column and lending it to the 3 in the U column, thus making the 3 into a 13).

Step 3:   '*... and pay back on the doorstep*' (this meant writing a small 1 on the bottom line next to the 8 in the T column).

Step 4:   '*7 from 13* (now counting on fingers 8, 9, 10, 11, 12, 13) ... *is 6.*'

Step 5:   (now working in the tens column): '*Add the 1* (the same 1 previously paid back to the T column on the doorstep) *to the 8 to make 9.*'

Step 6:   '*9 from 5 you cannot do so borrow one* (1) *from the top* (that is borrowing from the 9 in the H column, thus making the 5 in the T column into 15).

Step 7:   '*... and pay back on the doorstep*' (thus writing a small 1 next to the 6 in the H column.

Step 8:   (now working in the hundreds column): '*Add the 1 to the 6 to make 7...and 7 from 9 is 2.*'

Easy – the answer is 266. What a triumph!

Still confused? I'm not surprised. While as a child I could carry out the method, I never ever understood how you could borrow from one place and pay back to another. I mean just imagine if I had borrowed sixpence (6d/a tanner/half a bob) from my sister and paid it back to my brother – I doubt it somehow!

As an adult I can analyse what was going on, and try to second-guess why my teacher taught me this method of subtraction. Perhaps this was the way she had been taught to do subtraction, perhaps this was the method many of my peers were taught subtraction. However, recognizing my own confusion as a child serves to help me recognize, as an adult, the potential confusion today's children might experience. When given a method or an algorithm the 'right' answer may emerge but this does little in terms of helping children understand what is actually going on. What, fundamentally, is the mathematics a child is operating with? What at the most basic do they need to understand?

Mathematically, the method described above was a version of decomposition, but instead of having crossings out on the page (our teacher would never have tolerated such a slovenly approach to our doing our sums) we were carrying out a compensation method. So when I borrowed 1 from the 'top', and lent it as a 10 to the column to the right, the '1' is paid back in the same column to the number on the 'bottom'. This in fact is equivalent to the 'balancing' approach often used as a method for solving simple linear equations. Unfortunately it seems as though things have not moved on very much. We still have a flawed algorithm known as decomposition that children are expected to make sense of by suspending their mathematical belief system in order to accommodate the method and assimilate it into their schema.

Carrying out the same calculation as above, the current orthodoxy works as follows:

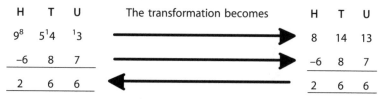

This method of decomposition is basically flawed on two mathematical counts. The first is one I alluded to above; to tell children they cannot take 7 from 3 (in the units column) is a mathematical untruth; a denial of life below zero. Of course we can take 7 from 3; the answer is negative 4. Secondly, using the method of decomposition, we frequently end up with amounts that cannot possibly exist, well not if we wish to preserve the integrity of the place value system. This is because the place value system (or as I prefer to describe it the value of the place system) is only intended to accommodate just one digit, ranging from 0 to 9, in each column. To suggest a two-digit number can be written in a column defies the whole system of place value.

To reiterate, any column within the place value system is only designed to accommodate a single digit. We cannot start lobbing two digits into a single column; this completely undermines the learning that young children engage with when they learn how the increase from 9 to 10 becomes a change from a one-digit number to a two-digit number. AS such another mathematical untruth is being carried out. On the one hand, children are being taught about how the place value system works, that once we count past 9 and get to 10, we must place the 1 digit in a 'new' column called the 'tens'; this obviously continues until we move from 99 to 100. On the other hand we are asking children to disregard the underlying structure of the place value system and to accept that we can indeed have a value greater than 9 in any column. Confused? We ought to be.

Apart from using the powerful method of counting on, perhaps making use of an empty number line, the only other algorithm I believe sustains mathematical integrity is based upon acceptance that there is life below zero and requires pupils to understand that counting backwards from zero we gain the values ⁻1, ⁻2, ⁻3, and so on.

Carrying out the same calculation as before, we can work either from left to right or right to left in the first instance; it does not matter. Working from left to right, in the hundreds column 9 take 6 is 3, in the tens column 5 take 8 is ⁻3 and in the units column 3 take away 7 is also ⁻4, as illustrated below:

H	T	U
9	5	3
–6	8	7
3	⁻3	⁻4
2	6	6

This line means 300 less 30 less 4.

This is gained from 300 – 30 – 4 (see below).

The beauty of this approach is that it not only maintains mathematical integrity, it also provides pupils with an opportunity to practise mental arithmetic. So, the 3 in the hundred's column is worth 300 and the ⁻3 in the ten's column is worth ⁻30. 300 and ⁻30 is 270. Finally 270 and ⁻4 (from the unit's column) produces the correct answer of 266.

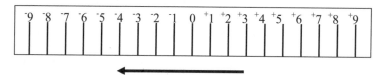

Furthermore, by providing pupils with access to a simple resource of a number line running from ⁻9 to ⁺9, all the possible values can be calculated. When a pupil is asked to calculate 3 take away 7, they can use a number line resource (below) to carry out the calculation; thus by counting back 7 spaces from ⁺3 we arrive at ⁻4.

I did not invent this algorithm for subtraction. I first saw it over twenty years ago in a volume of *Mathematics Teaching*, the journal of the ATM. The issue here is that despite such a robust method existing in the domain of school mathematics, why does it only rarely appear in classrooms? Could it be that the perceived orthodoxy of using the decomposition algorithm for carrying out a subtraction is unquestionable? Could it be that sometimes, just sometimes, the perceived orthodoxy might just be inadequate and therefore needs to be challenged and, when it is seen to be lacking, and in this case mathematically untruthful, changed?

Questioning orthodoxies

So, what else is there in the way mathematics is currently taught that might be worth questioning? Well, how about multiplication? For example, with regard to a question such as: 'What are 3 lots of 5?' Is the calculation 3 × 5 or is it 5 × 3 . . . and does it matter?

Diagrammatically 3 lots of 5 could look as follows:

It is irrelevant whether these three sets of five dots are drawn horizontally, vertically or in a random way. What is important is that, as a multiplication calculation, the arrangement is 5 × 3. This is because it is the function (× 3) that is operating repeatedly on an amount of five objects, thus 5 'times' 3.

At issue is whether it makes a difference to write 5 × 3 or 3 × 5. Mathematically, because multiplication is commutative and 5 × 3 will produce the same answer as 3 × 5, it may seem not to matter. However, this (commutativity) is the kind of knowledge an adult or an older student is likely to be comfortable with. As far as young children learning the concept of what multiplication means, I suggest it is vitally important that we do not 'take for granted' they will automatically understand commutativity on two counts. The first is that an important aspect of learning mathematics is about pupils constructing mental pictures and working with physical images in order to make sense of abstract concepts. Mathematics is largely something we do in our mind that we translate into pictures and symbols. We need to utilize imagery as a powerful tool in sense making. In this context, therefore, I believe it is important to enable children to construct pictures that accurately give sense making to mathematical operations. The alternative picture would have five lots of three objects, which is 3 × 5. Second, while as adults we take for granted that 5 × 3 gives the same result as 3 × 5, expecting pupils to take this for granted is done at their peril; this is because of the danger of children forming misconceptions that if 5 × 3 is equal to 3 × 5 then perhaps they can take for granted that 5 ÷ 3 is the same as 3 ÷ 5, which of course it is not. The question here is what can and cannot be taken for granted, what can and what cannot be generalized?

Commutativity, therefore, is a 'big' idea in mathematics and, as such, creating opportunities to enable pupils to explore which operations are commutative and which are not is a valuable part of teaching and learning mathematics. The following idea might be used with a Year 3 or 4 class and considers multiplication in the guise of the area of a rectangle. In the first instance I see the idea as a counting type task, which later provides opportunities for pupils to seek generality, that is that the area of a rectangle can be viewed as a function of multiplication.

Multiplication as a counting and an area type task

Draw a rectangle on square grid paper (say up to a maximum of a 10 by 10 square), so the bottom left-hand corner of the rectangle is drawn at a fixed point (see diagram below). Next, count the number of (1 by 1) squares inside the rectangle and write the answer in the top right-hand corner of the rectangle. Draw another rectangle, again placing the bottom left-hand corner at the same fixed point and writing the total number of squares, or its area, in the top right-hand corner. For example, if the first rectangle to be drawn has dimensions 6 by 3 and the next rectangle has dimensions 2 by 5, the following diagram should be drawn:

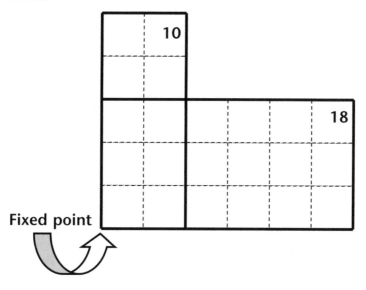

At different times in carrying out this task different pupils will recognize they do not need to keep counting all the individual squares in each rectangle they draw and instead may recognize they can calculate each answer using multiplication. There is an assessment opportunity here about whether a pupil can find a quicker way of working out the area of a rectangle other than by counting in 1s.

As more and more rectangles are added to the picture, lists of multiples emerge and pupils can produce a traditional 'table square'. The assessment opportunity is seeing how quickly any pupil shifts from counting to generality; looking for patterns in the completed table is a further stage. For example, a 6 by 3 rectangle will have the same area as a 3 by 6 (which generalizes to $m \times n = n \times m$). Clearly young children are unlikely to write such a generality but the important issue is to create situations that enable such patterns to emerge and for young pupils to construct verbal explanations of what they notice.

Division – equal shares or dividing into

Moving onto division, here is another concept involving similar complexities as follows. If we consider the calculation 15 ÷ 3, what exactly does this mean? If it means 15 shared equally into three groups, then pictorially it would look like the earlier array, that is:

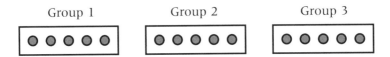

Here the answer is gleaned from the (equal) number of objects in each group.

However, if 15 ÷ 3 is interpreted as 15 objects divided into 3's, a different picture emerges, that is:

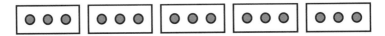

This second illustration is in fact the basis of 'chunking', where lots of 3's are taken away from the starting total (15) until zero is reached. Mathematically, 15 ÷ 3 is a fraction written as 15/3, and this creates the question: 'How many 3's are there in 15?' Thus, 'sharing into' is not the same as 'dividing by'; again there exists an inconsistency in pictorial interpretations of what the operation of division means. To reiterate the issue of children seeing or drawing pictures to depict mathematics is important; as such, children's pictures and mental images need to be consistent with the underlying mathematics.

I return to my earlier conjecture that telling and analysing anecdotes about the way we were taught is one way of exploring one's belief systems about mathematics and about how we might teach most effectively. Looking carefully at what we are telling pupils and being aware of the potential for them to develop misconceptions when they are given quick tricks in order to achieve answers are crucial aspects of planning and teaching.

The eleven-plus and all that rot

My second anecdote is less to do with learning mathematics and more about testing as a flawed way of assessing pupils' achievements. This time I return to my eleven-plus examination in 1960, the year Burnley were crowned League Division One champions by beating Manchester City 1–2 at Maine Road.

> I remember sitting in the examination room, terrified of the thought of failing and going to one of the secondary modern schools where I understood all kinds of terrible things happened. A lot of my friends had been told they would be given a new bike if they passed and my elder brother was already at the grammar school.
>
> I remember fearing to look this way or that; the most vivid memory was of a giant of a man telling the assembled testees that under no circumstances must anyone turn over the page until he told them to. I waited until this instruction was given. I was no 'slouch' and completed the first two pages with ease. Then I waited, and I waited, but nobody seemed to be telling me to turn over to the next page. There were only a few minutes left when I noticed an instruction at the bottom of the page reading:
>
> *Turn over to the next page*
>
> Contrary to others' expectations of me, I didn't, therefore, go to the grammar school; perhaps my saving grace was that I had done enough on the story and comprehension test to qualify me to go to Burnley Technical High School.
>
> September 1960 saw me dressed in a bright blue uniform, ready to begin my secondary school education, at Burnley Technical High School. I imagine that on the 'strength' of the eleven-plus results I was placed in 1D, the 'bottom' class for everything. I knew I wasn't 'dim' but increasingly accepted a bottom set mentality; and could frequently be found smoking with the 'toughest' of the fourth year boys behind the boiler house; after all I had to get my kudos from somewhere.
>
> Within the lessons I tried hard to show I wasn't unintelligent, and seemed to come close to the top in tests. I remember feeling, however, that even if I did come top rather than third or fourth, this would only get me into the C stream, whereas the 'really clever' people were even higher up in the B and A streams. All hope of

aspiring much beyond class D, to which I had been designated, appeared fruitless and futile. Despite having been considered one of the stronger pupils in my primary school, I stayed in the bottom stream for three years. The most important part of school life was to pass around the football team lists during those lessons immediately before playtime; we did not wish to lose time picking teams in our own time. The bell goes, out we would dash, coats down, teams line up, kick off, bliss.

Issues of fear are raised here; of passing or failing a stupid test, of making simple mistakes under the pressure. Failing to recognize the effects such mistakes can have upon individuals' aspirations was, and continues to be, inexcusable. Creating an education system grounded on results of testing at age 11, to provide information about pupils' aptitudes, to support the process of transfer from primary to secondary school was abhorrent. The fact this system continues today, through dressed up in slightly different clothes of 'national tests' should be a cause for concern at the highest level of government.

Informing and developing pedagogy

This fear and abhorrence of testing and my subsequent placement into a low-ability stream was to have a profound influence upon my development as a teacher. As a head of mathematics from 1986–1995, I worked with department colleagues to develop ways of teaching and assessing pupils' achievements that were not based upon tests, and which did not require us to set pupils by so-called ability. Fortunately, I had a marvellous headteacher, Peter Hampson, who was fully supportive of my desire to work in mixed-attainment groups. However, he was not prepared for me to base the mathematical education of the pupils in the school upon socio-political or socio-educational beliefs; he also made it clear that he would only support my desire to move to mixed groups if this approach resulted in an improvement in the way mathematics was taught and learned and in GCSE results. This issue, of the importance of the nature of the support senior managers provides for staff and the whole-school ethos they seek to create, is something I have already discussed in the previous chapter. What I experienced was support founded upon a desire by the headteacher to improve the way mathematics had formerly been taught and for pupils to gain a more positive view of mathematics.

As a result of being failed by the system I sought, therefore, through my interactions with pupils, to boost confidence, to create an environment founded on the pleasure of learning and to reduce pupils' fear of learning mathematics. Of course the eleven-plus no longer exists in most parts of the country. It has, however, been replaced by Key Stage 2 national tests and, just as fifty years ago, the results of the tests are often used to allocate pupils to sets or streams. As such, current generations of children's educational futures are in danger of being determined by a couple of tests they take in the month of May at the age of 11 ... just when there are more important things to be doing such as 'playing out'.

Is it any wonder, therefore, that some parents who choose to prioritize some of their earnings undergo a yearly scrabble to find people who will give their children individual tuition in order to increase their children's chances in national tests and, accordingly, their life opportunities? I do not in any way wish to be critical of such parents as I have given tuition myself. They have a fundamental right to choose what is best for their own children's education and, therefore, how to make best use of their disposable income. Ultimately they are, after all, only responding to a government agenda that places such high stakes on testing and ability grouping as mainstays of its education policy. I am, however, critical of governments that have based the education of millions of children upon deeply flawed policy dressed up in the name of 'standards'.

The central theme of this chapter has been about reflection upon personal learning experiences in order to analyse current approaches to teaching. As a teacher I can sense when things are going well in a classroom; I can equally sense when things are not going so well and that I need to change something. If, through the process of reflecting upon a lesson, I can analyse what the elements were that caused a lesson to be 'successful', I can seek to bring such elements to future lessons. Likewise I can analyse elements and events that leave me feeling uneasy about a lesson (or a continuing professional development session with adults). The key indicator rests with engagement and while there will always be some who will engage positively, there can often be others who, for whatever reason, rarely do so. The indicators I look for are based upon the critical mass of pupils and delegates and if the messages I receive from this critical mass tell me things are going OK or, even better, that they are engrossed and interested in what they are doing, then I can take great encouragement from such information.

Reflection and analysis are skills that can serve us well in our professional development and, as teachers of mathematics, help us rationalize the ways we teach, the resources we use and the cultures we seek to create in our classrooms.

Learning mathematics through exploration 4

Being an explorer at any level and of anything is essentially about seeking answers to questions; about the desire to find out and make sense of the social and physical environments in which we exist. In this sense, to some extent, everyone is an explorer. Exploration, the desire to find out, is, I suggest, a common and very powerful human characteristic; something that binds us and drives us. Because exploration is such a motivational force it seems to make good sense to use such a force as the basis for learning and teaching mathematics.

Through exploration we not only find answers to the questions we ask, we sometimes find answers to questions which, at the time, we may not have been looking at or looking for. Thus, some of the major discoveries of our time (Fleming and penicillin, Röntgen and X-rays) have been discovered by 'accident'; learning is, in part, analogous in microcosm to such major discoveries. One of the challenges for teachers of mathematics is to enable pupils to become explorers and problem solvers. Solving a range of problems in non-obvious or unfamiliar contexts is at the heart of mathematical activity, as borne out by Cockcroft (1982, paragraph 231):

> In recent years there has been considerable discussion of the nature of mathematical understanding. There is general agreement that understanding in mathematics implies an ability to recognise and to make use of a mathematical concept in a variety of settings, including some which are not immediately familiar.

This notion of being an explorer of mathematics is closely aligned to 'discovery' learning, a notion discussed in the Plowden Report (1967), and the following quotation (paragraph 549) aptly sums up the issues of discovery learning or exploration:

The sense of personal discovery influences the intensity of a child's experience, the vividness of his (sic) memory and the probability of effective transfer of learning. At the same time it is true that trivial ideas and inefficient methods may be 'discovered'. Furthermore, time does not allow children to find their way by discovery to all that they have to learn. In this matter, as in all education, the teacher is responsible for encouraging children in enquiries which lead to discovery and for asking leading questions.

This chapter, therefore, is about how we can cause pupils to learn mathematics by helping them become explorers of mathematics. Some initial questions might be:

- Why might we want pupils to become explorers of mathematics?
- How might we cause pupils to become mathematical explorers?
- How might we encourage pupils to work hard on a problem that does not appear to have a simple or quick solution?
- How might we encourage pupils to go for depth and quality, rather than them seeing mathematics as a race or as a process of carrying out a quantity of 'sums'?

Underpinning each of these questions is the issue of teaching mathematical content knowledge through, and simultaneously with, pupils developing skills of processing mathematics.

Processing content

In the first three iterations of National Curriculum (from 1989), process skills were described as a separate, discrete attainment target and, in order to assess pupils' levels of Ma1-type achievements, this frequently led to Ma1 being taught in a fragmented, bolt-on way, where 'investigations' were given to pupils in different types of lessons in comparison to mainstream mathematics lessons. The difficulty with this approach is because Ma1 are processes, it becomes artificial to teach and assess pupils' Ma1 type skills in isolation to and outside of content-focused contexts; that is, mathematical processes are not, in themselves, mathematical content. Mathematical content needs to be processed for it to make any sense to the learner.

For a simple analogy, one might consider a tin or a packet of frozen or dried peas. The peas are the content and the process is the way the peas have been preserved, so the peas can be eaten months after they have been harvested. Assessment of the effectiveness of the process is whether the contents can in fact be eaten several weeks/months later ... something we may have Napoleon to thank for or perhaps Nicolas Appert! So the story goes, when Napoleon's army suffered more from malnutrition than from Russian musket balls, he offered a prize of 12,000 francs to anyone who could find a way of preserving food. This prize went to Nicolas Appert who theorized that food would be preserved if it was stored in airtight containers and heated up appropriately. Thus, the process of canning and sterilizing was created.

Just as the peas are the content that require processing (unless they are bought and eaten fresh from their pods), so Pythagoras' theorem, trigonometry, transformations and indeed all mathematical concepts make more sense to pupils if they are learned as an outcome of being provided with an opportunity to process, or to explore, such concepts.

Fortunately, in the fourth version of the National Curriculum, Ma1 was integrated into each of the other attainment targets (Ma2, Ma3 and Ma4). Subsequently, in the latest version of the curriculum teachers have been given positive encouragement to weave problem solving, communicating and reasoning into their teaching. This approach supports the development and use of more open-ended tasks that encourage teaching approaches where pupils are enabled to learn mathematical content and simultaneously develop problem-solving skills.

To illustrate this issue of processing content I offer three situations. The first is a problem that would be suitable, in the main, for pupils in the 9–12-year-old age range, the second is suitable for students in the 12–15-year-old age range and a third suitable for students in the 15–18-year-old age range. Despite offering these broad age-related categories, I am usually cautious about ascribing specific problems to particular age ranges. As teachers we constantly have to make decisions about where the problems we offer might be used for the first time in a scheme of work. Thus, the three example problems/tasks to follow would, in my long-term planning, respectively be written into schemes of work covering Key Stage 2/early Key Stage 3, Key Stage 3/ early Key Stage 4 and Key Stage 4/early Key Stage 5. Of course 'rich mathematical tasks' such as the ones I describe will be suitable for exploration in some form or other across different age ranges. How any teacher decides to use or adapt a task for different classes is an important aspect of professional decision making.

The first is a well-known problem often called 'snook'. It has certainly been around a long time so I was somewhat astonished when, upon introducing it to some mathematics teachers recently, only two out of the eight had met and used it before.

The basic idea is to start with a rectangle drawn on squared paper. A 'mathematical' billiard ball begins a journey at corner A and proceeds along a 45° diagonal path until it either reaches another corner or another side, at which point (if it reaches a side) the ball rebounds at a 90° angle. This process continues until the ball exits at one of the corners.

In the example below, with a 5 by 3 rectangle, the journey ends at corner C.

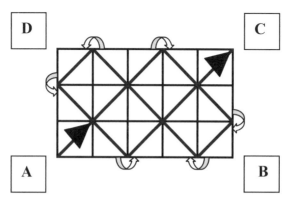

One way I have used this problem is to ask a class what other information, beyond the finishing corner, they might gather from this diagram. Some suggestions have been:

- How many rebounds are there?
- How 'long' (in terms of diagonals) is the path?
- How can the path be described?
- What different shapes are made in the diagram and what are their areas?

For a 5 by 3 rectangle, the answers are:

- Six rebounds
- 15 diagonals long
- 3, 2, 1, 3, 1, 2, 3
- Four squares of area 2, six triangles of area 1 and two triangles of area ½.

Pupils can now explore this situation by gathering some or all of this information for different sized rectangles.

A question for a teacher choosing to use this problem might be: 'What content is being processed by getting pupils to work on this problem?' For the situation above where the dimensions are co-prime (that is, the highest common factor they share is 1), the length of the route (measured in number of diagonals) is 15.

The areas of the shapes, while simple to calculate, must total up to 15; in this case we have four lots of 2, six lots of 1 and two lots of a ½ creating the calculation: $2 \times 4 + 1 \times 6 + ½ \times 2 = 15$. Knowing the dimensions, therefore, provides a useful checking mechanism for correct calculations of the sum of the areas of the shapes.

The description of the journey is symmetrical about the middle value in the seven parts of the journey (3, 2, 1, 3, 1, 2, 3); recognizing the emergence of symmetry within a numerical context is an important aspect of mathematics.

Finally, each move of the journey could be described using vector notation. So the first move in the example is a $\begin{bmatrix} 3 \\ 3 \end{bmatrix}$ vector.

Having described each of the other moves, these vectors can be totalled and the result should be the single vector $\begin{bmatrix} 5 \\ 3 \end{bmatrix}$ which, in turn, are the dimensions of the rectangle and, therefore, the vector from the starting to the finishing corner.

The value of utilizing this type of problem is that different content areas can be engaged with, in an interconnected way, and each content area is worked on in a problem-solving type context. Thus, the content skills and knowledge to be used and applied (processed) emerge in a purposeful way. Developing pupils' problem-solving skills is, I suggest, the most singularly important, functionally academic purpose that education serves per se. Here is a list of the mathematical concepts, therefore, that pupils can engage with as a consequence of exploring this problem:

- factors and highest common factors
- area
- symmetry
- vectors.

The second exploration is intended to engage students with concepts of angle and centres of rotation and requires them to have access to squared paper (preferably 2cm squares) and tracing paper. Using the diagram below as a starting point, the task is to seek centres of rotation so an image of square A fits exactly on top of square B.

This is clearly a closed task. There are exactly three centres of rotation and to find these centres students are likely to use a trial and improvement approach. The exploration, however, is one of developing the task by changing the relative positions of squares A and B in order to seek a generality about how the three centres are determined according to the positions of any two squares.

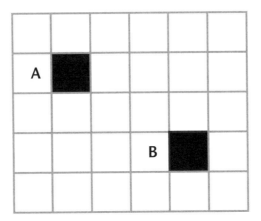

The mathematical content knowledge up for grabs is:

- The three centres of rotation are co-linear.
- The line joining the centres is the perpendicular bisector of a line joining the centres of the two squares.
- The centres of the squares and the two outer centres of rotation form the corners of a new square.
- If these four points are described using coordinates, then a further exploration can be carried out to find how the coordinates of the two outer centres of rotation connect to the centres of the original squares A and B.

Finally, as with the previous problem, a vector description could be applied to the sides of the new square and so we have another problem-solving context for developing students' knowledge and using and applying vectors. You can find a version of this task in *100+ Ideas for Teaching Mathematics* (Ollerton: 2007).

The third task is intended to enable students to explore the fundamental basis of trigonometry and is, I believe, the most powerful approach to understanding this complex concept. The explanation below describes a scenario that is far from being an 'open-ended' investigation, but neither is it intended to be. What I want students to do is to explore a situation and develop this exploration through a sequence of guided questions, each of which are intended to cause them to discover mathematical truths for themselves, rather than me, as their teacher, having to tell them what they need to know in order to understand a concept. There are rich opportunities for students to explore and to make sense of the information they collect.

I have two different starting points to offer. The first is for students to make their own rotating arm grids using card, square grid paper, some glue and a split pin. The second is to provide students with a copy of a sheet similar to the one in the diagram. The second approach enables students to access the ideas more speedily, though this may be at the expense of them gaining greater ownership of the work as a consequence of having created the rotating arm themselves. The student sheet is a coordinate grid from 0 to 1.0 on each axis and has part of a protractor superimposed so that the 0° (and 180°) measure lies on the x-axis and the 90° measure lies on the y-axis.

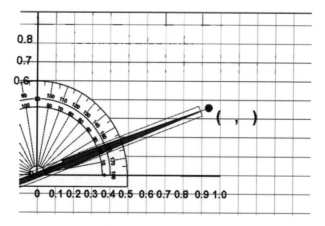

I set up the 'mini' exploration as follows:

I draw a line, which I later refer to as a 'rotating arm', inclined at, say, 20° to the horizontal and 1 unit in length (or 15cm) and ask students to make an estimate of the coordinates of the end of the rotating arm. Thus, for a line inclined at 20° the x ordinate would be in the region of 0.94 and the y ordinate would be approximately 0.34. Students are now set the task of repeating this scenario for other angles, in multiples of 10° and from 0° to 90°, and estimating the *x* and *y* ordinates for the end of each line.

Having completed this task (and students will naturally achieve this at different paces), I pose a sequence of further questions such as:

- Look at your results and write about any patterns you notice.
- When will the answers in the H and V columns, (the *x*, *y*) coordinates, be the same?
- Why do you think the answers are the same at this point?
- Estimate the results (to 2 places of decimal) for the following pairs of angles:
  a) 27° and 63°
  b) 35° and 55°
  c) 42° and 48°.
- Compare your answers with another person's answers and discuss what you see.
- Look at your results and write about what you notice.

At this point of the exploration students are constructing trigonometric tables for cosine and sine functions for angles from 0° to 90°. The importance of this approach is that the values that emerge do so from a measurement-type task that students have derived for themselves and therefore can take ownership of. This, in turn, has a more profound impact upon learning than the one I experienced as a youngster where these tables were presented to me as a *fait accompli* and I did not have the foggiest idea of where they had come from or what they meant.

The following question will act as an extension for some students:

- Without drawing any further lines (rotating arms), estimate coordinates for angles of 110°, 150°, 200°, 250°, 290°, 330°, 360°.

Seeking to answer these questions engages students in determining when ordinates have negative readings and thus the notion of angles in different quadrants can emerge.

The next questions are intended to help students see connections between the information they have previously collected and the information contained within their calculators:

- Draw another table of angles from 0° to 90° and, for each angle value, press the cos and the sin keys on your calculator.
- Round each of these answers off to 2 places of decimal.
- Compare the two sets of results and write about what you notice.

As students complete these tasks my intention is for them to see for themselves how the trigonometric values from their calculators are the same as, or very close to, those they have already collected from the rotating arm grid.

Some further leading questions based upon students writing the calculator sequence they would need to use for each of the following situations where the length of the rotating arm is something other than 1 could include:

If the rotating arm was:

- 2 units long what would happen to the x and y ordinates?
- 3 units long what would happen to the x and y ordinates?
- 2.5 units long what would happen to the x and y ordinates?
- 3.7 units long what would happen to the x and y ordinates?
- 20 units long what would happen to the x and y ordinates?

There is still a lot more development work for students to do in order for them to see how all this exploration can lead to an understanding of one of the more challenging concepts within GCSE syllabi. Some developments are:

- For students to draw examples of these situations in the form of right-angled triangles.
- For the teacher to explicitly introduce the vocabulary of opposite, adjacent and hypotenuse. These words need to be carefully defined, particularly 'opposite' and 'adjacent' in terms of what any side is opposite or adjacent to. The importance of getting the students to fully understand this terminology is that the same side of a right-angled triangle, other then the hypotenuse, can be described as being either opposite or adjacent and this depends upon the angle under consideration.
- To ask students to pose their own problems on square grid paper and to check their answers by measuring.
- To ask students to pose their own problems on plain paper and to check their answers by measuring.

Students can begin to engage with graphical aspects of sine and cosine functions, for example:

- Without further use of a calculator, work out the coordinates of the end of the rotating arm for every angle starting at 100° up to 360° (in 10° intervals).

Draw graphs of:

- Angle against x ordinates (to create the graph of the cosine function) and angle against *y* ordinates (sine function) for all angles from 0° to 360°.

- Plot these graphs on the same pair of axes.
- Write about the shapes of these graphs.
- Find all the places where these two graphs cross.

Each step requires students to explore deeper and deeper into the concept of trigonometry, though I have purposefully not even begun to help students develop connections, as yet, between sine, cosine and tangent. In my planning this becomes yet a further development.

To finish, I offer some thoughts about the original questions I posed at the beginning of the chapter.

Why might we want students to become explorers of mathematics?

I believe we are all explorers of all manner of situations. This is because we are fundamentally inquisitive beings. We seek answers to questions and solutions to problems. Life is about coming across, and trying to solve, problems. This is the case in many social interactions, in tasks we carry out either professionally or as amateurs, or in our pastimes. If enquiry were not such a strong human characteristic, then there would have been little drive to 'invent' the wheel and Google would have been but a flight of fantasy in the minds of heretics. As such, by setting up puzzles and problems, of whatever magnitude, for students to explore is to tap into their natural inclinations and patterns of behaviour. Using this innate desire to enquire provides therefore a most effective way of supporting students' mathematical learning. I have discussed this issue in Chapter 2.

How might we cause students to become mathematical explorers?

Encouraging students to explore situations, to ask or construct questions, as well as seeking answers to puzzles and problems is a clear pedagogical decision a teacher makes. This is about creating a questioning, enquiry-based culture. To develop such a classroom culture, I chose to weave this kind of approach into lessons on as frequent a basis as possible, beginning in lesson one with a new class.

In order to develop the kind of culture I sought, I believed it was important to pose a problem as soon as students entered the room. Rather than try to explain what my expectations were about, how I wished them to work or to explain my objectives, it was more valuable to offer students a problem that would automatically draw them into the world of problem-posing/problem-solving mathematics and let them see and feel for themselves what being in 'my' mathematics class was all about. No need to explain my objectives because these would become self-evident. Furthermore, and because there exists an inexhaustible list of such problems, it was easy to plan such problems into students' mathematical experience. Publications that form part of such a list can easily be found in catalogues produced by the ATM, Tarquin, Claire Publications and the 'nrich' website.

How might we encourage students to work hard on a problem that does not appear to have a simple or quick solution?

Developing mathematical 'doggedness' in students is clearly not easy, particularly if some students' previous experience has taught them that mathematics is about producing right and wrong answers in response to short, closed questions. Developing in students a determination to stick with a problem and not to give up if an answer does not quickly emerge is something that needs to be constantly worked on, and again as soon as they enter our classrooms. Developing students' positive attitudinal attributes of stickability, a willingness not to 'give up' and being able to cope with 'stuckness' are important personal qualities. Of course, for how long any student will be able to stay with and try to work through a difficulty will vary for individuals; this is as much about differentiated states of learning as it is their ability to understand concepts and the different work rates they bring to their classrooms. The key issue here, however, is seeking to develop a classroom culture where learning attitudes and, in particular, mathematical attitudes are seen by the students as more important than being the first to get ten correct answers to ten sums. This leads me to my next question.

How might we encourage students to go for depth, rather than seeing mathematics as a race?

The issues here are similar to those discussed in the previous paragraph. The difference lies in developing students' understanding that learning is about depth of understanding, in contrast to seeing mathematics as a race where the first one to get all the 'correct' answers is seen as the 'best' in the class. One of the more important aspects of classroom culture, I felt, was to encourage students to develop an idea in depth, irrespective of what other students were doing or how fast or how far others had been able to develop a problem. This approach was about getting students to compete with their own intellectual development, rather than competing with others in the class. In sporting contexts this is referred to achieving one's 'personal best' or PB. Indeed, because one aspect of this deepening process is about asking students to teach one another or to explain what the next stage is in the development of a problem, this creates a collaborative approach to learning mathematics. Using the trigonometry example above, there are a range of development steps, each taking students deeper into the concepts I intended them to engage with. Of course, how far anyone got and to what depth anyone developed a task was dependent upon students' interest, motivation and stickability.

To conclude this chapter I suggest that discovery learning or exploration is the most potent way of teaching because the focus is more upon students' learning. This is about balance, which leads me appropriately or perhaps conveniently into the next chapter – the balance between teaching and learning.

The balance between teaching and learning 5

A radical transformation occurs in the classroom when one knows how to subordinate teaching to learning. It enables us to expect very unusual results from students – for instance that all students will perform very well, very early on...

Gattegno (1971, ii)

In this chapter, I consider some of the complexities and challenges that teachers face day by day in classrooms. I explore how teaching impacts upon students' learning and how teachers might go about planning and carrying out their lesson plans with minimalism in mind; how the interactions they have with whole groups and with individuals' leads to change in students' mathematical understanding.

The quotation above, taken from *What we owe children: the subordination of teaching to learning* by Gattegno (1971), is what this chapter is fundamentally about. Determining how learning can best be fostered so students are provided with opportunities to use their natural, innate talents in order to accommodate, assimilate and develop knowledge and understanding is complex. Learning is messy and unpredictable; it needs to be challenging and worth doing; learning also needs to be accessible and achievable.

'Passing on' knowledge

As a young teacher I cannot remember whether I had a desire to pass my knowledge on to my students. I suspect not because at the time I did not think I had much knowledge. I was certainly not confident or assured about any mathematical knowledge I did have or which was worth passing on. Given my track record of failing the eleven-plus, scraping together six O levels over three years (five of them at the lowest possible grade) and gaining zero amount of A levels, neither did I have a sense of the 'worth' of any knowledge I might have had. I mention this because, as a teacher trainer, I have heard many interviewees, when applying for teacher training courses, express their reason for wishing to become a teacher as 'I wish to pass on my knowledge to others'. My thoughts in response to this kind of pronouncement inevitably were:

- Whether the knowledge they had was worth 'passing on'.
- Why potential teachers have a perception that teaching is about the passing on of their knowledge.
- If teaching were about passing on knowledge, we would end up in a downward spiral of knowledge; like 'Chinese whispers' information becomes reduced, distorted and minimized.

Of course the opposite is the case. Evolution ensures knowledge increases. For example, the ease of access to the world wide web has enabled an explosion of knowledge. How accurate some of the knowledge is and what anyone does with any knowledge, whether it is used for benign or malignant purposes is another matter. What is certain is the next generation of school children will have access to far more knowledge and have more ways of engaging with and using that knowledge than the current generation ... and so on. How future generations process and interrogate any knowledge is of far greater importance than accepting knowledge as truth.

Teaching, therefore, is far more than finding ways of passing on knowledge. It is about organizing learning so students feel confident to try ideas out, look for connections, seek opportunities to be creative, be analytical, construct generalities and take the initiative. As such, teaching must, in some ways, be subordinated to learning. Broadly speaking, the role of the teacher is to help students develop skills of organizing, analysing and generalizing.

Seeking a balance

To develop this issue of balance between teaching and learning I use a question from John Mason:

> Have you ever found yourself talking, telling pupils things, and wished
> that somehow things were different, that they were doing the work?
>
> Pimm (ed.) (1988: 164)

Well, have you? I certainly have and all too often I have
compounded the difficulty by continuing to 'teach'. I recognize
the conditions, however, when I do not subordinate my teaching
to students' learning. This is when I am doing too much talking
and the students are doing too much listening or not listening,
whichever the case might be. I also know how uncomfortable I
begin to feel as I realize that what I am saying, accompanied with
increased amounts of hand waving, appears to be having little
impact upon those I am teaching. Even worse, I know I am not
reaching the students. I also know I am working too hard and
those I am supposedly 'teaching' are not working hard enough
. . . how do I manage to end up in such an impasse? The key word
here is 'working' and the central issue is about who is doing it?

A simplistic image I use to describe this state of affairs and one
that often springs to my mind's eye is one of a see-saw. I see the
teacher on one end and students at the other, in a state of
imbalance, that is:

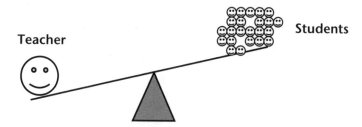

When I am doing too much of the talking for too much of the
time then the see-saw becomes out of balance; the students
become passive receivers of information. Trying to recognize for
myself when I am doing too much talking requires me to develop
and hone the skill of metacognition; the skill of seeking to
become aware of how I am teaching and what modes of teaching
I am utilizing while I am in the throes of teaching. This is not an
easy skill to develop, particularly when up to the eyeballs in
making on-the-spot decisions; not just about how I am teaching
but also how students are responding. Though metacognition or
recognizing what I am doing, in the moment, is not an easy skill
to explicitly develop, it is something I can work on in order to
help me develop my practice.

To strike a balance there needs to be times when the teacher is seemingly taking a 'back seat', so the students are doing the work. I say seemingly because teaching is all too often regarded as some kind of 'performance'. However, there is obviously far more to teaching than that which occurs while teacher and students are occupying the same classroom space. Teaching is also about what happens before a teacher enters a classroom; that is the planning they put into as lesson. Teaching is also about making ongoing assessments. While the former takes place (usually) when the teacher is not in the classroom, the latter, the most effective and dynamic form of assessment, occurs when the teacher and students are together in the same room. This puts some of the marking we do outside the classroom into a stark perspective.

In any classroom, students need to have opportunities to learn how to do more of the running; simply put, they need to learn how to learn. In a mathematics classroom, students need to be provided with tasks that cause them to process whatever content knowledge is on offer. This requires students to be provided with ideas that, as mentioned earlier, they are expected to develop, analyse and explain what sense they have made of a problem. To redress the balance depicted earlier by the see-saw, I need to find puzzles and problems that:

- won't take me an inordinate amount of time to explain
- enable students to begin working fairly quickly
- are both accessible and extendible.

Below I offer two examples of tasks that meet these criteria.

A problem that is suitable for, say, Year 6 pupils, yet could easily be adapted and simplified for a Key Stage 1 group or made more complex for a Key Stage 3 group, is one I call 'pebbles'. Pupils could be given four pebbles to weigh in the first place. Alternatively, they might be given a slightly more abstract version with pictures of four weights. Here is the slightly more abstract version.

> With weights of 3.1kg, 1.2kg, 500g and 200g, what other weights can be made by using different combinations of these?
> Further questions could be:
> Have you found them all?
> Can you place each result on a scale from 0kg to 5kg?

This problem, provided in whatever form, is intended to provide pupils with opportunities to:

- search for all possible solutions (of which there are 15)
- order information
- explain why they think they have found all solutions.

In terms of generality, this latter task could be used to engage pupils in the mathematics of permutations. The immediate mathematical content on offer is:

- working with different units of measure
- placing different measures on a scale
- addition
- working with decimals (depending upon the initial values suggested at the outset of the problem).

A development of this problem would be to use a pair of balancing scales that, in turn, will engage pupils with subtraction by finding the difference between two amounts. So, if on a pair of balance scales we place the 3.1kg weight on one pan and the 500g weight on the other, then a weight of 2.6kg (or 2600g) will be required to create a balance. This problem is a relatively closed one, yet the important criteria is that the task is relatively easy to explain and to set up.

The next problem, to do with angles and similarity, also fulfils these two criteria, but it also offers students opportunities to develop the task to greater depths. The starting point is something as simple as drawing two lines on a rectangular piece of paper, such that one line goes from the top to the bottom side (though not into a corner) and the other line goes from the left-hand side to the right-hand side, again not into a corner. Having drawn these lines, a problem for, say, 14- or 15-year-old students could be to explain why (to prove) the shapes A and B are similar and shapes C and D are similar.

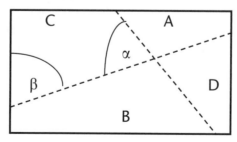

One approach to this problem could be to cut out the shapes and match pairs of corresponding angles for each pair of shapes A and B, C and D. This, though, is a demonstration rather than a proof. The other, more definitive method of proof, would be to label an angle at the centre as, say, α and an angle at the edge as, say, β and work out all the other angles in terms of α and β; the equality of corresponding angles will become apparent.

A development of this task could be to consider what different numbers of sides can be produced when two lines are drawn from side to side, side to corner or corner to corner. These will produce combinations of three-, four- and five-sided shapes, for example:

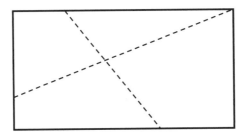

In this diagram above there is one three-sided and three four-sided shapes and in order to work out all the angles, in term of α and β, the student will need to be utilizing generalized angle facts. By drawing any two straight lines in a rectangle, it is possible also to produce different diagrams: for example, two four-sided and two three-sided shapes, three three-sided and one five-sided shape, and there are still others to be found. Expecting students to work on how many 'different' sets of shapes are possible and then trying to prove all possible results have been found will provide a further challenge.

Again, the problem takes very little time to set up yet involves students in much mathematical machination. How much further input any teacher offers any individual will, of course, vary enormously. How any input is offered will depend upon whether the teacher decides to encourage students to work together in order to give support to one another.

Helping students to learn to collaborate is one aspect of working on the balance between teaching and learning. A second aspect relates to helping students' develop responsibility for their learning. I develop these two issues below.

The collaborative classroom

Getting students to work collaboratively in groups is more likely to be successful if they have an expectation that variety is what happens with their teacher in their classroom. The implications of this relates to what happens when meeting a class for the first time. Setting out one's expectations about, for example, working collaboratively is going to be easier to do at the outset than trying to set up a collaborative work ethic several weeks or months in to a teacher's relationship with a class. This may sound obvious, yet how many times do we attend a course then try out a 'new' strategy with an 'old' class and wonder why it is not perhaps greeted with the same enthusiasm with which you met the idea on the course? This can be debilitating. Of course, if a class is perfectly used to their teacher trying out new ideas and students expect to see different furniture arrangements when they enter the room, they are more likely to accept change; this can only be beneficial to them as learners.

Finding tasks that students can easily see the benefit of collaborating on will enable them to value such ways of working. There is clearly a difference between students sitting together in a group and working as individuals, and sitting together as a group with the purpose of working as a group. When a group of people contribute to the greater good of each individual's benefit in that group, this sounds like Socialism. I prefer to call it common sense, sharing and kindness.

One useful motivator for students to work in a group occurs when a task is shared out, so not everyone needs to do everything; instead they can combine their efforts and as a consequence gather more information about a task than had they worked individually.

I believe it is useful for students to have fluency with mathematical 'building blocks' and become confident with the knowledge they gain. This is because fluency, confidence and knowledge are three important and interconnected strands in children's mathematical development. With this belief in mind, therefore, I want to set up tasks that enable these strands to be developed. I illustrate this with four examples, one taken from work that could be used with Key Stage 2/3, two ideas about revision techniques for KS4 students and finally a task for use with Key Stage 5 students.

A group-work task for Key Stage 2/3 students

Knowing how to calculate the divisors of numbers is one aspect of the 'fluency, confidence, knowledge' triad. Taking the focus of divisors, therefore, as the mathematical content to be developed with a class, the following task can be organized where everyone can contribute and everyone can gain from each others' contributions.

The idea is for groups of six students to work together, initially in three pairs, thus enabling discussion and to offer mutual support. Each pair calculates the divisors of 20 of the numbers between 1 and 60; the teacher might utilize Post-it notes for pairs of students to write the divisors of their allocated 20 numbers on. Once this task has been completed the six students can come together to share their information, perhaps putting all 60 Post-it notes, now containing the divisors of each number, in numerical order.

The next phase of the task is to distribute a sheet looking something as follows, which individual students can fill in, taking information from the Post-it notes.

Number	Divisors	Amount of divisors
1		
2		
3		
4		
...		
...		
59		
60		

A final task could be to make a display, using 60 pieces of card in three different colours. On one colour all the numbers with an odd amount of divisors are listed, on another colour all the numbers with exactly two divisors are listed and on the third colour are all the rest. Clearly this is a task to highlight the square and the prime numbers = 60. Once all the cards have been filled in there is a clear opportunity to create a display that can be referred to not only by the students who have worked on the task, but by students from other classes as well. In this way such a display can be used as a resource or as a reminder about divisors of numbers.

Two tasks for revision purposes for Key Stage 4 students

The context for the next two tasks relate to developing revision strategies. The first requires the teacher to identify areas of the curriculum they believe a certain group of students (for example those on the GCSE grade C/D borderline) would benefit from having further input about. Having chosen three or four specific topic areas, preferably connected in some way, the following process can be organized for students to work on over the course of a lesson. The idea is for students to work in groups of threes, so how many areas of the curriculum are chosen will partly depend upon the number of students on the C/D borderline there are in a class. This organization might take place in the last few minutes of a lesson with the intention that students can carry out some research on the web (for homework) between this and the following mathematics lesson.

If, for example, we decide upon three topic areas such as expanding brackets, factorizing a quadratic and graphing quadratics, the idea is to turn small groups of students into 'experts' at one of these areas of mathematics; to ask them to work together and finally to disseminate and share their collective knowledge. Each group is given one of the topics to a) research and b) decide how they are going to explain what they know to two other people. Research, in this instance, means finding out how to carry out a specific mathematical procedure. To do this, they might draw upon:

- existing personal knowledge
- www
- textbooks (if a department uses them)
- each other.

This means students in each small group are expected to take responsibility for collaborating in order to be able to share their collective knowledge and consider how they are going to teach other students later in the lesson.

For the first 20 minutes, therefore, students work together in their groups to develop and share their knowledge. In the final 30 minutes the students re-form into different groups of threes so there is one student from each different topic area. The idea now is for each student to explain to the other two what they have learned about their specific topic area. This is repeated within the same newly formed groups so everyone has had an opportunity to do some peer teaching and everyone has an opportunity to learn from their peers.

The second idea is where the teacher chooses three questions from past papers, again that focus on similar areas of the mathematics syllabus and that students would benefit from concentrating on. The students are asked to write their answers to the three questions in test conditions and are given 15 or 20 minutes to answer them as fully as possible. The next part of the strategy is for students to form groups of three in order to share their solutions with each other. The final part of the strategy is for the teacher to invite individuals to explain how they worked out different parts of each question; students can explain how they tackled each of the questions both successfully and the kind of mistakes they made. By the end of the lesson, students should have access to 'model' solutions, as well as being aware of the kind of mistakes commonly made.

A group-work task for Key Stage 5 students

This task is aimed at developing students' fluency, confidence and knowledge of sine curves and some of its derivatives. Where exactly this task needs to start from will obviously depend upon the knowledge a teacher understands her students are already confident with; in this instance, I am assuming students have all drawn the basic sine curve and know how it has been derived in the first instance. Pairs of students work together and have access to grids with the basic sine curve drawn on, that is:

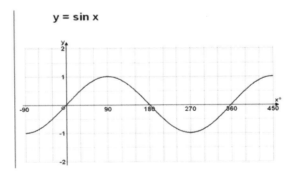

On this grid students work out and superimpose one of the following eight graphs:

$y = 2\sin x$ $y = \tfrac{1}{2}\sin x$ $y = \sin 2x$ $y = \sin \tfrac{1}{2}x$
$y = 2\sin 2x$ $y = 2\sin \tfrac{1}{2}x$ $y = \tfrac{1}{2}\sin 2x$ $y = \tfrac{1}{2}\sin \tfrac{1}{2}x$

Each pair of students can draw four each of the above graphs, so when two pairs of students come together to share their work they will have all of the above eight graphs drawn and each one superimposed on the basic sine curve. A group discussion is intended to focus on what transformations have taken place and why, and under what conditions these transformations have occurred.

The second aspect, referred to earlier, of helping students to develop responsibility for their learning cannot, of course, be wholly separated from issues involved in setting up collaborative learning opportunities. However, encouraging students to become responsible learners is something that needs to be planned for and worked on.

Helping students develop responsibility for their learning

Developing personal responsibility is complex. Being responsible is not a fixed or a permanent state; I am sure I am not alone in recognizing occasions when I have failed to take responsibility or have made bad decisions. Trying to guide those we teach, therefore, to recognize the value of accepting and becoming evermore responsible learners is even more complex. However, somehow or another we largely learn to conduct our lives in responsible, rational ways. Whether one person's degree of responsibility is perceived by another to be 'acceptable' or is lived out in rational ways is a matter of personal judgement; subjectivity abounds.

In classrooms, teachers are faced with the unenviable task of working with students from a wide range of home backgrounds where different modes of behaviour are tolerated and encouraged (or discouraged); where degrees of taking personal responsibility are encouraged (or discouraged). We know, however, that the more responsibility students take for their behaviour and their learning, the more they will get out of school and the more successful, in whichever way this is measured, students become. This is the case whether students' educational achievement is acted out on a sports field, on school trips, in a corridor or in the classroom.

In classrooms, these are some of the characteristics responsible learners might display:

- They have a go at a problem and do not give up the moment a difficulty arises.
- They develop problems beyond an initial starting point.
- They analyse information they have collected themselves or which they have been presented with.
- They seek generality, thus going beyond the production of face value answers.
- They see value in communicating their work to others in the class, either verbally, in the form of a poster or a report.

Here are two problems that provide opportunities for students to engage with the characteristics in the list above. The first is taken from an Association of Teachers of Mathematics (ATM) publication, *Points of Departure 3*, and is called 'Sums and products'. The problem is as follows:

> Choose a number and partition it in different ways.
> For example, if the chosen number is 8 then some partitions could be:
> $1 + 4 + 1 + 2$
> $5 + 3$
> $1 + 2 + 5$
> $1 + 1 + 1 + 1 + 1 + 1 + 1 + 1$
>
> Next change each of the addition signs into multiplication signs and work out the product so formed.
> $1 \times 4 \times 1 \times 2 = 8$
> $5 \times 3 = 15$
> $1 \times 2 \times 5 = 10$
> $1 \times 1 \times 1 \times 1 \times 1 \times 1 \times 1 \times 1 = 1$

From this data the highest product is 15; the problem to solve is:

- What partition, when turned into a multiplication calculation, will create the highest product?

This problem is ripe for development beyond the starting point described and to do this students will not only have to look for a higher product resulting from partitioning the suggested number (8 in this instance), but will consider partitions and products for different starting numbers. This in turn leads students to search out patterns arising from working with a range of starting numbers and their resulting maximum product. Seeking a general result and trying to explain why their generality, or generalities for this problem, hold true is a key feature. Each step enables students to deepen their understanding of the underlying structure revealed. Some students may develop the problem even further by relaxing the rule of partitioning into whole numbers; thus a partition of $2.5 + 2.5 + 3$, which becomes $2.5 \times 2.5 \times 3$, which equals 18.75, is a larger product than the one using whole numbers only. (But is there an even higher product?)

The next problem is taken from another ATM publication, *Learning and teaching mathematics without a textbook* (Ollerton: 2002), and is called 'Do we meet?' It has an accessible starting point for Key Stage 3 students and has built-in developments, some of which would challenge A-level students. The problem is based upon movements on a square grid by two people, A and B. A and B are on two different grid points and the idea is for person A to move in such a way, when person B moves twice as far in the same direction ($\times 2$ SD), person B meets up with person A. Person A moves first and usually they make a move 'towards' person B. However, the solution requires some counter-intuitive thinking, as revealed in the example game below:

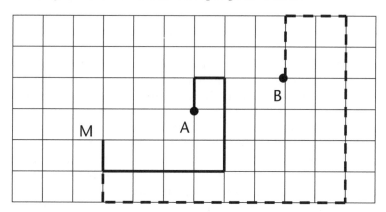

Asking students to see how to arrive at a meeting point (M) when points A and B are placed in different positions on the grid usually leads to some of the following conjectures:

- Points A, B and M always lie on a straight line.
- The distance between A and B is equal to the distance between M and A (or the distance between A and B is half the distance between M and B).
- The path from B to M is a × 2 enlargement of the path from A to M.

The teacher might encourage the use of vector notation here, by suggesting students consider the vectors AB, MA and MB.

Extensions are many:

- What happens if person B moves three times as far in the same direction as person A (× 3 SD)?
- What happens if person B moves twice as far in the opposite direction to person A (× 2 OD)?
- What happens if person B moves the same distance and at 90° (clockwise) to person A (× 1 RA)?
- What happens if person B moves twice as far and at 90° (clockwise) to person A (× 2 RA) and as mentioned above?
- A challenge for A-level students is what happens if person B moves at any other angle of direction and any scale factor to person A?

Developing any problem depends on two central issues. The first relates to the nature of the problems on offer. Problems must have some degree of open-endedness, where parameters are understood and variables can be changed. The second issue is connected to students' expectations of what their mathematics lessons are largely about. If they develop an expectation that tasks are rarely closed or have opportunities for creative thought and the possibility of extension, then this is how they will learn to operate. This is a further example of developing a culture of learning.

In this chapter, I have considered the issue of the balance between teaching and learning and have offered tasks that are intended to create a balance between how much work a teacher does, in terms of didactic passing on of knowledge, and how much work the students do in terms of making sense of the mathematics on offer. Of these tasks, two require minimal input from the teacher, three require the teacher to organize a collaborative approach to learning and two focus on students' developing a task and, therefore, taking greater responsibility for their learning. Clearly, it would be nonsensical to suggest that mathematical tasks can be classified in ways that match criteria of minimal teacher input, collaborative working and developing students' responsibility. However, what I have sought to raise is that each of these approaches to teaching are key aspects of supporting effective learning.

What any teacher's aims are when they plan their lessons will determine what tasks to offer and in what ways they intend to organize their students' learning; this has implications for resources and classroom organization. What is important is that underpinning each of the tasks is an underlying principle about the role of the teacher; this, in part, is about 'lighting the blue touch paper and retiring'. Of course, the teacher does not completely distance herself from the action. She will constantly be available to intervene and offer support and encouragement where necessary. The role of the teacher, however, is not about filling the students with knowledge, whoever it may belong to, but rather it is about subordinating their teaching to their students' learning. This, in turn, requires attention being paid to the balance between teaching and learning.

Models for teaching mathematics 6

In the December 1992 journal, *Mathematics Teaching* (MT141), there is an article by Alan Wigley titled 'Models for teaching mathematics'. When I occasionally bump into Alan, usually at the ATM Easter conference, I mention this article as one I find interesting and ask him if he ever thinks about developing it in the light of all the changes that have occurred in mathematics teaching since 1992; that is before the inception of national strategies. This chapter is based upon this article and I seek to offer my own slant on the issues of teaching mathematics through two alternative models Wigley describes as the 'path-smoothing' and the 'challenging' models.

I begin by taking a quotation from the article in order to set the scene for the remainder of this chapter.

> There is a tendency in debate to polarize teaching and learning styles into one of two camps:
>
> | | |
> |---|---|
> | exploration | instruction |
> | invented methods | given methods |
> | creative | imitative |
> | reasoned | rote |
> | informal | formal |
> | progressive | traditional |
> | open | closed |
> | process | content |
> | talking (pupil) | talking (teacher) |
> | listening (teacher) | listening (pupil) |
>
> The standard response is to declare oneself to favour a mixture of methods, neither entirely didactic nor entirely exploratory. But it is precisely here that the danger of cosy consensus lies. The problem is not *whether* one should use a mix of methods (of that I have no doubt) but precisely *how* the blend should be achieved.

This article informs my pedagogy for teaching mathematics; it helps me become more explicit about aspects of mathematics teaching I intuitively engage with yet may not have previously had the words to describe. Learning to become explicit about the implicit and conscious of the instinctive is, I believe, an important aspect of professional development. Coming to know what our pedagogy is, becoming clear about the beliefs and values we hold and which drive us, and being able to articulate them helps underpin effective practice.

Polarities and the politics of choice

I too am interested in spectrums and polarities. Life is often described in terms of 'black and white' yet rarely do we live life at the poles. Generally we inhabit 'grey areas', frequently having to cope with ambiguity and complexity. All too often debate is polarized; we typically hear politically charged, adversarial discussion in the media such as the Radio 4 *Today* programme. So it frequently is with teaching mathematics. Some people refer to mathematics as a 'right or wrong' type discipline yet I challenge this perspective, believing instead that mathematics does not need to be reduced to such a simplistic, reductionist perspective. Likewise, I do not believe there are definitively 'right' or 'wrong' ways of teaching mathematics; there may be effective and less effective ways to teach mathematics but these constructions must be for individual teachers to determine; ownership and autonomy are incredibly important aspects of professionalism.

A key issue is the need for degrees of choice about how to determine ways of teaching mathematics in more effective ways than might be cascaded down via government quangos, local authority consultants and national strategy writers, and checked by teams of inspectors. There often grows a perceived orthodoxy about how to teach, for example by writing objectives on the board or by following advice about how to plan and order approaches to teaching.

Sadly much of this advice is all too frequently aimed at getting teachers to make their students jump through hoops and to enable them to gain more marks on national tests. This, in turn, is so politicians can use data from test results to show their policies are 'working'. Thus, what is used as a measure of a successful mathematics education is illusionary; we know, deep down, the moment many students leave the examination room much of the information they took in with them and the tricks they used to answer questions are also left behind. Furthermore, the way information is gathered and the way tests are conducted, with students working individually, is not the way most of us operate for the vast majority of the time. Communication is a marvellous thing; collaboration essential.

A far more valuable measure of any person's mathematical capability is when a student uses and applies mathematics to solve a problem in a non-obvious context or when they make choices about how to work on a problem, such as whether to work individually or with others. To illustrate this point I draw upon a problem I first met when reading a seminal text called *Starting Points* by Banwell (1972) et al. If you ever get the chance to buy a copy of this publication, perhaps on eBay, then snap it up for it is sadly out of print, but never, ever, ever lend it out – it may not come back!

This problem is about joining dots and creates opportunities for students to organize the way they work and explore number patterns that arise. My adaptation of the problem is as follows:

By placing five dots (or tiddlywinks) in a straight line there are four joins.

By arranging the five dots as below seven joins can be made.

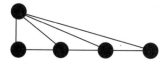

Joins are straight lines, though not necessarily the same length.

If all five dots are arranged in the shape of a pentagon, ten joins can be made, which is the maximum number of joins possible for five dots.

The problem is to find other numbers of joins for five dots, six dots and so on.

- What is the second highest number of joins for different numbers of dots? I ask about the second highest because the highest will, of course, be a value in the triangular number sequence.
- What numbers of joins are not possible?

Gathering, organizing and analysing information is not something that a timed test can accommodate. However, by observing how students work on such a problem, the teacher will be able to see how they organize themselves and what sense they make of the problem. Students might be encouraged to work individually in the first instance and later share and compare their information, both to check their results and to discuss what occurs. In this way, students will have opportunities to use and apply mathematics, such as how systematic and how organized they are. Of course, the complexity is how such achievement can be measured and recorded. It is because any 'real' or valuable measure of student achievement is so complex that inadequate tests are used instead; thus reductionism of marks and levels rules.

Challenging and path-smoothing

In my mathematics classrooms, which nowadays is either working in other teachers' classes or with adults, for example, teaching assistants, trainee teachers and mathematics teachers, it is my intention to engage those present with mathematics as a challenging, mind-boggling, 'a-hah' type discipline. I seek to offer situations that encourage problem solving, to cause questions to be asked as well as questions to be answered. Tasks and problems are intended to focus thinking on and develop an understanding of skills and concepts, where aspects of 'stuckness' as well as moments of insight and illumination can be experienced.

There are times, however, when I actively choose to smooth a path, particularly if I become aware of frustrations building up that may lead to the possibility of either the problem itself being rejected or the problem solver feeling less good about mathematics than I would want them to.

I might also choose to smooth a path if I am not entirely sure of my ground, as I found myself recently. I was working with another teacher's class and, therefore, I knew little about the dynamics of that teacher's classroom and even less about any of the pupils. My next anecdote, therefore, is about teaching another teacher's class and describes a situation where I chose to adopt a path-smoothing approach with a hint of exploration and problem solving, just to add a semblance of challenge.

Planning to teach long division

I had been asked to carry out some curriculum development work that focused on pupils engaging in problem-solving approaches to learning mathematics in three primary schools in south-west Cumbria. This project involved working with staff over three twilight sessions and teaching two days in each of the three schools. The teaching involved working with each age group from Reception to Year 6 over the six days; given that teaching Reception-aged children is well beyond my past experience and my comfort zone, I had some trepidation. My loving partner meanwhile made gleeful comments about me being 'found out' for the impostor I was! The project itself, however, was right up my street in terms of using problem-solving approaches to learning and teaching mathematics.

Coming out as I do in a pedagogical rash at the notion of doing 'demonstration' lessons, I sought to ensure that whatever I brought to other teachers' classrooms was something they could work with themselves; not to replicate something I do, but instead to consider some of the underlying principles apparent in the ideas I bring to their classrooms. I wanted colleagues to consider how the approaches I offered might be adopted and adapted into their practice. In each lesson, therefore, I asked the class teacher to join in once I had completed my initial input; after all, it was their pupils' experience of how they responded to being taught in problem-solving type ways that was of paramount importance.

During one lesson I was asked by a teacher if, for the next lesson, I could plan an investigative way of teaching long division, particularly as he was concerned about his Year 5 pupils' lack of success with the 'chunking' method he had previously used. I was aware of similar comments, about the chunking method, having been made by several (at least a dozen) other primary teachers and teaching assistants, so this was not an uncommon event. Having been posed this challenge, my first thought was that ... *long division is about as interesting as watching paint dry*. Nevertheless the request had been made and I was keen to respond positively.

The challenge for me was to try to find an investigative approach that would support pupils' learning of a narrow and not very exciting skill. At the point of the question being posed I had no idea how I might respond to the request in a way that would allow me to maintain my pedagogy and also rise to the challenge in a professional manner.

I had therefore to return to my own basics, to consider my first principles, which are:

- My intuitive approach to teaching is to encourage learners to explore situations.
- As an outcome of pupils' engagement with a puzzle or problem I offer, I want them to see self-evident mathematical 'truths'.
- I want, at all costs, to avoid explaining an algorithmic process and then to ask pupils to practise the algorithm until they become 'expert' at using it.

In order to try to put these principles into practice, I needed to understand current orthodoxy which is to use the method of chunking that involves pupils working out multiples of the divisor, then carrying out several subtractions from the desired starting amount. As mentioned above, I had been told by several teachers how difficult and arduous they find it is to explain the method of chunking and, in turn, how difficult their pupils find it to carry out the algorithm, both when it comes to the subtraction part of the algorithm and then having to keep track of exactly how many chunks of the divisor they have subtracted. It is, in fact, quite a complex procedure. Thus, it was against this backdrop I set about looking at how to plan an alternative way of 'teaching' long division. I wanted to find an approach that pupils could make sense of for themselves without me providing small step-by-step instructions.

'Teaching' long division

At this juncture I need to refer to one of the most powerful mathematical systems ever constructed and, what is more, one which does not, I feel, receive the attention it deserves; this is the binary system. I believe there is enormous 'power' (no pun intended) in the binary system despite or, perversely, because it is not given much houseroom in the National Curriculum or any of the strategy documents. I have spent some time teaching binary to pupils from Year 4 to Year 11. The binary system is inordinately powerful, basically because the whole of our digitized technology has its roots in the binary system. I also recalled, somewhere in my dim and distant past, a vague memory of using binary arithmetic to do calculations. I set out to try to utilize this system in order to help pupils explore long division as described below.

For the calculation 594 ÷ 27, which is equal to 22, we can use a system of doubling as follows:

$27 \times 1 = 27$
$27 \times 2 = 54$
$27 \times 4 = 108$
$27 \times 8 = 216$
$27 \times 16 = 432$

Supposing, I asked myself, I gave the pupils the numbers {27, 54, 108, 216, 432} and asked them to find out which of them they would need to use to make a total of 594?
  These would be 432, 108 and 54, so as above:

$$432 = 27 \times 16$$
$$108 = 27 \times 4$$
$$54 = 27 \times 2$$

Collecting these multiples of 27 together we have (16 + 4 + 2) 'lots' of 27, which falls out as 27 × 22.

The whole of the process, therefore, can be reduced to:

- carrying out an initial calculation of 27 × 1
- doing some repeated doublings (of 27)
- carrying out some addition.

However, I did not merely want to give the pupils this method as this would be to replace one algorithm with another, albeit I believe, much more robust, usable one. I wanted instead to find a way of enabling pupils to construct or develop this method through an exploratory approach. With these intentions I produced the puzzle (below) and, with nothing more than a 1-minute introduction, I handed out a copy of the sheet and asked them to work with a partner to try to find out what was going on. I actively chose to offer no further explanation or input; I had already worked hard enough doing the thinking and the planning; now it was the pupils' turn to do the work.

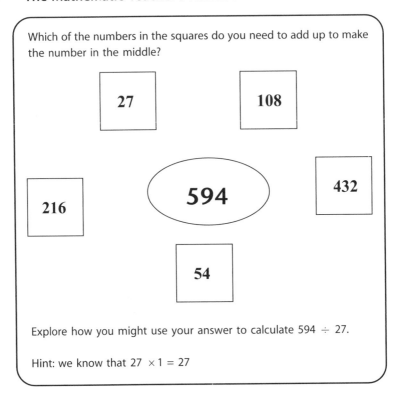

Which of the numbers in the squares do you need to add up to make the number in the middle?

27

108

216

594

432

54

Explore how you might use your answer to calculate 594 ÷ 27.

Hint: we know that 27 × 1 = 27

I purposefully chose not to give any explanation to the pupils because I intended the method to become self-explanatory, particularly as a result of asking pupils to work together to solve the puzzle. I also did not wish to smooth the path too much so I chose not to write the values in the squares in sequential order (that is 27, 54, 108 and so on). Both of these proved to be useful strategies because within 2 or 3 minutes some pairs of pupils had worked out what was going on and asked me if I had another one for them to do.

I had prepared several other sheets, the second containing slightly less information than the first and the third containing even less. The final sheet asked pupils to construct a question, work out their answer and then give their question to someone else. What I did not do, though would in a similar circumstance, was to ask pupils to try this method out on someone at home – I always think it is valuable to put pupils in the position of 'teacher'. A further development could be to choose values where the denominator does not divide exactly into the numerator, so leaving a remainder.

Sheet 2 read:

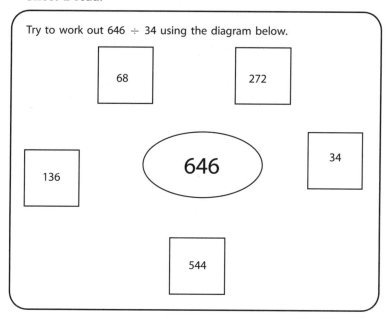

Try to work out 646 ÷ 34 using the diagram below.

68

272

136

646

34

544

Sheet 3 read:

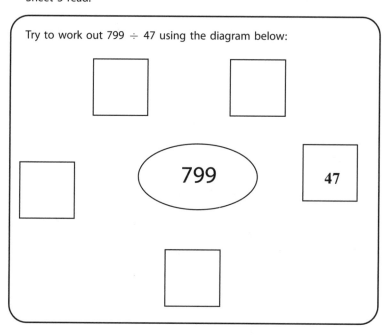

Try to work out 799 ÷ 47 using the diagram below:

799

47

A fascinating situation emerged as pupils completed one sheet after another and by the end of the lesson some pupils were literally pleading with me to give them another long division calculation to work out. There were several reasons behind their pleas. I believed they arose because:

- Pupils had worked something out for themselves that had not required them to follow my specific method or algorithm.
- Pupils were being successful with something they had previously found difficult and uninteresting.
- There was only one puzzle/challenge on each A5 sheet of paper; thus pupils were not faced with a whole set of questions from an exercise to work through.
- The success they gained and the sense they were able to make of the tasks helped pupils develop their confidence.
- The confidence pupils gained through their success helped them develop competence with long division.

The outcome was one very pleased teacher, one relieved author (as I had not tried this idea out before) and pupils who had become far more confident at being able to carry out a calculation they had previously struggled with.

I was keen to ascertain if this method might be translated into another teacher's practice so I sent the idea to Zoe, a NQT who I had had the pleasure of working with during her training year. Below is the response Zoe sent in an email:

Hi Mike

I did long division with my Year 6 the other day. Amazingly pain free! Starting as a puzzle, then discussing what we have done meant they seem to be able to do it, can explain what to do and were pleasantly surprised. 'What, is that it?' said one of my least confident children. I think I was most impressed when they could explain it the next day and apply it to a 'normal' question – that is presented just as 434 divided by 19 or whatever.

Some also independently observed, that, rather than adding totals you could take them away – this was noticed on an example like 527 divided by 17:

17 × 1 = 17
17 × 2 = 34
17 × 4 = 68

17 × 8 = 136
17 × 16 = 272
17 × 32 = 544

Most noticed that 544 was too big and added all the rest up but some (interestingly across ability range) noticed that 544 was only 17 more than the target and so calculated (32 − 1) lots of 17 = 31 lots of 17.

I think the trick is that all they have to do is to double and add. When we did 'chunking' before mistakes tended to be made either when multiplying by 3 and so on and when generating a list of facts (only those more 'mathematical' generate lists with obvious easy totals, for example, 10×, 2×, then doubling or halving to make more totals). They also make mistakes when subtracting. However, my pupils are secure with adding and doubling though I am sure they are not unusual in that. So not only was the idea successful in itself but also provided a very useful confidence boost (for one boy in particular) at a crucial time.

Thanks a lot

Zoe

The remainder of this chapter is based upon analysis of some of the items in the earlier lists (p. 63), looking at achieving a blend of ways of working rather than seeking a 'cosy consensus'.

Exploration and instruction

In the previous chapter I wrote about the value of students being provided with situations to explore; what is important here is to discuss the role of instruction within exploration. Instruction can take two broadly different forms:

1. Giving students a set method for calculating for instance a missing side in a right-angled triangle, or the transmission approach.
2. Describing a process for students to carry in order for them to 'arrive' at Pythagoras' theorem through exploration.

Considering in the first instance the transmission approach, of the teacher explaining what steps students must take to apply Pythagoras' theorem, I am sure I am not alone in recognizing the frustration of having to repeatedly explain the same process over and over again and still 'they don't get it'. No matter how carefully and how slowly I offer explanations, when the need to use Pythagoras' theorem emerges later in the term, when we have moved onto a different topic, why do so many students appear clueless and unable to not only recall how to use the theorem, but even to recognize that it might be an appropriate time to use it? Frustrations abound. If, on the other hand, I set up an exploration that requires students in the first instance to follow a process and, having carried out the process, are then invited to make sense of the resulting information and construct the formula for themselves, I am more confident students will remember the theorem and recognize when to use and apply it.

The process that I allude to works as follows in the example below:

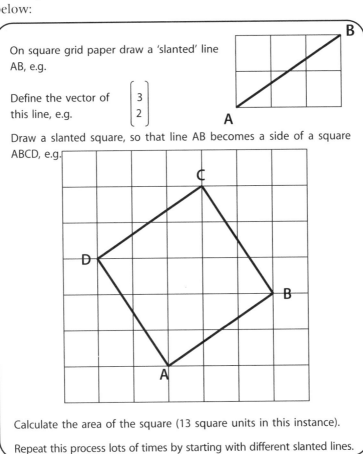

On square grid paper draw a 'slanted' line AB, e.g.

Define the vector of this line, e.g. $\begin{bmatrix} 3 \\ 2 \end{bmatrix}$

Draw a slanted square, so that line AB becomes a side of a square ABCD, e.g.

Calculate the area of the square (13 square units in this instance).

Repeat this process lots of times by starting with different slanted lines.

Of course, groups of students can collect information and share their results.

By looking for a way of connecting the vector of the slanted line with the area of the slanted square, students will in effect be carrying out Pythagoras' theorem. There is, of course, still a long way to go before students may fully appreciate this connection, which includes them:

- getting to grips with the associated vocabulary
- seeing how the connection works for non-integer values
- using the connection to calculate one of the two shorter sides of a right-angled triangle
- applying their knowledge in three dimensions.

All of this takes time and for this reason I anticipate students work on a module, with the slanted line and slanted square task as the starting point, for at least three weeks; thus enabling depth of understanding.

Invented methods and given methods

The issue here depends upon what knowledge I have as teacher with regard to activities I offer students to enable them to understand a mathematical truth. In the previous example, students are being encouraged to discover for themselves the connection between the sides of a right-angled triangle, rather than me giving them this connection. Because I have 'slanted squares' in my knowledge bank of tasks then I draw upon it when I want students to learn about Pythagoras' theorem. However, when it comes to teaching the concept of the area of a circle using the formula $A = \pi r^2$, I may decide to give students this formula, then check it out by asking them to draw various sizes of circles on 1cm-square grid paper and counting areas. I am, therefore, asking them to check out the validity of the formula by drawing and counting. Alternatively I could take pupils through the procedure of cutting up a circle into say 16 equal sectors then reforming 15 of the pieces and two half pieces into an approximate rectangle. However, I feel this is a particularly convoluted approach that, in my experience, students do not always find easy to follow. Perhaps I am just not very good at explaining it this way.

What is important is to develop students' expectations about the value of seeking connections, inventing methods and explaining what they have discovered; this is in contrast to me explaining, step by step, what I think they need to know. While students are not discovering something new to the world at large, they are discovering something for themselves; it is this process of discovery, followed by an explanation of what they have found, that leads to deeper understanding. Once students gain a deeper understanding of something, the more likely they are to retain that knowledge and be able to transfer it, use and apply it, to other contexts.

This approach, of students constructing knowledge through the process of discovery, can be applied to all aspects of school mathematics. Another example is described in Chapter 4, where students construct sine and cosine tables, without needing to know anything about trigonometry. The skill of the teacher is finding access points to concepts; tasks for students to engage with in order to reveal mathematical truths and to help them make sense of underlying mathematical systems and structures.

To quote Sotto (1994: 59):

> When we discover something ourselves we have direct experience of it. This knowledge is encoded inside us in a compacted, abstract living form, that enables us to grasp its meaning ... However, when someone tells us something, we do not need to strive to grasp its total meaning. We can simply memorize the words. That often gives us the illusion that we have understood.

The foundations of sense making, about anything, arise from learners having first-hand experiences. No matter how much teacher-telling takes place, understanding depends upon learners having opportunities to see for themselves how something works. A key role of the teacher is to find and offer tasks that enable students to access knowledge as an outcome of engaging with these tasks.

Reasoned and rote

I describe the notion of rote learning in two ways. The first is that of giving students 'tricks' or 'short cuts'. This is often aimed at trying to help students get the 'right' answers to questions, particularly in response to exercises from textbooks or with national tests in mind. This approach to teaching is in contrast to helping students get 'underneath' concepts so they build firm foundations for their future mathematical understanding. My second description is about practising a skill over and over again, aimed at developing students' fluency and, therefore, their confidence in mathematics. However, practising something the students have already reasoned out for themselves is different to them practising something they have been told 'works', as they may not understand how and why it works.

This business of learning by rote and learning the underlying concepts that give meaning to what has been learned by rote is a fascinating area for consideration and I develop this further in Chapter 8. For now I offer an example from my own practice as a secondary teacher.

The earlier example of developing students' knowledge of Pythagoras' theorem, by asking them to set up and solve a sufficient number of their own problems, once they have constructed the formula for themselves, is a valid way of helping them become fluent with the theorem. The approach I have used when asking students to set up and solve problems works as follows:

Pupils draw right-angled triangles, initially on 1cm-square grid paper. Assuming the two short sides of each triangle are of integer length they then apply the formula to calculate the length of each hypotenuse. Having written their answers to 1 decimal place they measure each hypotenuse with a ruler to check the relative accuracy of their initial calculation. Students can repeat this procedure a sufficient number of times until they are confident about how to apply their constructed formula; this is one basis of practise and consolidation. A further stage is to draw right-angled triangles on plain paper, thus students can work with non-integer length values for all three sides of the triangle. How many times each student will need to carry out the procedure in order to become fluent and confident with the formula will vary for each individual; this is one aspect of differentiated learning. A further extension would be to set up and solve problems in three dimensions.

Open and closed

Open-endedness is strongly aligned to curriculum differentiation and though the notion of working on 'open-ended' or investigative tasks has become a more commonly used phrase,

I wonder how often they are used in classrooms. Investigations or open tasks are mentioned in the Cockcroft Report of 1982, though they were around many years before (for example, *Starting Points* and *Points of Departure*, books 1 and 2, both published in 1972). Other excellent texts and resource books produced, which draw upon mathematical thinking and more open investigative work, include *Thinking Mathematically* (Mason et al: 1982) and *Thinking Things Through* (Burton: 1984). There is an excellent collection of puzzles and problems left to us by the late Gill Hatch titled *Leap to it, Jump to it, Bounce to it* and *Race to it* (originally published by Manchester Polytechnic, Didsbury School of Education, now Manchester Metropolitan University, 1984).

Sadly, the intention for more open, investigative work in classrooms was largely hijacked by examination boards, via the assessment agenda. As a consequence rather limited and narrow, closed GCSE coursework tasks were spawned, complete with mark sheets and answers! Fortunately, this type of coursework, or 'cursework' as I came to name it, has rightly been kicked into touch. Perhaps as an outcome of such nonsense we might see the rise of more pedagogically sound mathematics educational thinking.

Cockcroft was followed in 1985 by HMI *Mathematics from 5 to 16* and close on its heels in 1987 was *Better Mathematics*, a project led by Afzal Ahmed. The first National Curriculum *Non-Statutory Guidance* appeared in 1989. Each of these reports in turn supported the use of more open-ended tasks and questions in order that students were given a greater range of ways of learning mathematics by comparison to the more closed type approach of didactic teacher exposition followed by 'page 27 exercise A' in the textbook. It was not until 2004 that Adrian Smith's inquiry *Making Mathematics Count* was published and while this report does not offer explicit definitions of what constitutes effective teaching of mathematics, it does offer the following: 'Mathematical training disciplines the mind, develops logical and critical reasoning, and develops analytical and problem-solving skills to a high degree.' (2004: 11).

Seeking to define what is meant by an open or a closed problem would appear necessary at this point; as ever, in this age of postmodernism, I can only offer different ways of looking at the issue rather than a definitive answer. I see two different strands. The first is about the nature of the tasks and problems a teacher offers to students. The second is about how students are encouraged to consider different ways of solving a problem.

Considering the first issue I see problems that are more open than others, in comparison to some problems that are decidedly closed. A simple example of a closed problem could be, 'What is 4 multiplied by 9?' Here a specific answer is looked for. A more open alternative could be to 'What different pairs of whole numbers when multiplied together equal 36?' Although the latter question is more open than the first, it is effectively closed as there are a fixed number of known solutions.

Considering the second issue, if the question 'What is 4 multiplied by 9?' were to be followed up by students exploring patterns in the multiples of 9, where they have to make decisions about what to explore according to what they notice, the same closed question is being used in a different kind of way. Again, a specific answer is being looked for but this result is being used to check patterns and subsequent predictions in the multiples of 9. There are two patterns to be observed in the answers. One pattern is the tens digit in the product is always one less than that number of multiples of 9 in the original multiplication. So n multiplied by 9 (for $n < 10$) produces a 'tens' digit of $n - 1$. The second pattern is the value of the tens digit added with the value of the units digit (in the product) is always equal to 9. Similar, but different, patterns emerge for multiples of 9 between 11 and 20.

Similarly, in the approach to teaching Pythagoras' theorem offered above the 'answer' $(x^2 + y^2 = h^2)$ is clearly a 'closed' result; the approach used, however, is more open in as much as students are given a brief to explore a situation. How they do this will vary, both in their approaches to controlling variables and the speed at which they work on the task.

This issue of how many variables exist in a problem and how students are encouraged to work with and control variables is perhaps a useful way of thinking about how open or how closed a problem is. A good example is the group of problems involving areas and perimeters of rectangles. By keeping the area (A) constant, different dimensions, lengths (x) and widths (y) can be created and, thereby, different perimeters. By graphing length against width the graph $y = A/x$ can be produced. By keeping the perimeter (P) constant, different lengths and widths will produce different areas so the graph of length (x) against area (A) will produce a quadratic curve; meanwhile length against width will produce a linear graph of $x + y = P/2$. As an extension task a problem often called 'equitable rectangles,' where the value of the perimeter of a rectangle measured in centimetres is equal to the area of the same rectangle measured in square centimetres, can be explored. A further extension, which would bring in even more variables, would be to consider the area of shapes other than rectangles.

There is the potential for a massive amount of exploration here with many opportunities for students to control and change variables and look for connections. While there are fixed 'answers' to each problem, there exists a great amount of open-endedness enabling different students to develop the initial task to different degrees. It is in this regard that open-endedness is strongly aligned to differentiated learning.

> Mathematical content needs to be differentiated to match the abilities of the pupils, but according to the principle quoted from the Cockcroft report, this is achieved at each stage by extensions rather than deletions.
>
> (HMI, 1985: 26)

Supporting differentiated learning, therefore, requires the use of tasks that have degrees of open-endedness so everyone can make a start on a problem and there exists built-in extension opportunities that can be offered to more confident, higher-attaining students.

Talking (student), talking (teacher) and listening (teacher), listening (student)

These are the final two categories in the list at the beginning of the chapter and I am going to consider them together, I trust for obvious reasons. At issue here is what kind of talk is going on and what purpose any such talk is intended to achieve, with regard to teaching and learning mathematics. I feel sure we often wonder what happens between the time when we have taught our students something and what they ended up learning, or not, as the case might be. I have all too often and too easily laid the blame on lazy, unlistening students rather than considering what part I played in this developing scenario. From my perspective I have perhaps not been sufficiently explicit, at times, when I needed to be. At other times, however, I may have thought I was being clear, lucid and explicit but what I was talking about may have had little impact upon what students learned. I am not seeking to beat myself up here. However, identifying some of my less effective approaches to teaching can help me consider how I might become more effective. Analysing the type of talk teachers engage in is useful and I offer the following main aspects of teacher talk:

- explanatory
- confirmatory
- questioning
- offering an instruction
- setting up a task
- responding to the work students do (or don't do).

How and when I use any of these modes of talk will clearly depend upon a range of variables; some I can plan and prepare for, others, however, will be in response to unpredictable, unplanned events.

Below are some reflections I wrote about an event that occurred when I was temporarily teaching in another school. I offer it not to suggest that one form of practice is 'better' or more effective than another, but in order to consider the role of talk in mathematics classrooms.

I was teaching a Year 9 class. The general 'buzz' in the classroom, the occasional off-task remarks I found myself making to different students, the responding smiles and the 'general' sense that the students were applying themselves well to the tasks were all signs that the classroom was an OK place for us to inhabit. During the course of the lesson there were two occasions when I had to pop next door, to another room I also taught in, to get a couple of resources. Here the teacher was sitting at the front desk and all the students were working in a pin-dropping silence. I automatically assumed a test situation was taking place (there was a lot of testing carried out by the department) and I apologized for my intrusion. On the second occasion the same scenario was evident; on this occasion, however, I noticed the students were not in fact doing a test but were answering questions from an exercise in their textbooks. Each time I returned to my classroom I noticed the difference in the atmosphere and I wondered what the teacher next door would have made of my practice had s/he entered my classroom.

A key issue to emerge from this anecdote is the nature of the talk and how effective it is to support students' learning. Apart from 'silent' classrooms, I assume in many classrooms there is some talk that is of an off-task, social nature. Of course, significant difficulties can arise when such talk outweighs more purposeful mathematical talk, certainly if it becomes low-level disruption by nature, leading to an environment where effective learning is less likely to be taking place. When encouraging student discussion, therefore, the balance between productive on-task talk and disruptive off-task talk is an issue that needs to be considered.

As is the case with so much of what constitutes 'teaching', there are delicate balances to be negotiated. Perhaps it would be easier to insist students work silently. However, given the following short piece of writing, which emerged from a conversation with a secondary student who was keen to talk about her experience of discussion in her mathematics classrooms, there would appear to be a downside to such an approach.

> My maths teacher likes to be in complete control of a class. This is understandable to a certain degree, but he forbids us to talk unless specified otherwise. Now this is OK when he says 'I'd like no talking during this test', obviously this is fine, but then he takes it too far and won't let us talk full stop. At the beginning of an exercise, say from a textbook usually, he will say, 'No talking, I want to hear you concentrating'.
>
> This I find extremely annoying. I sit with two boys on a desk for three, and we are all great friends. We have a really good time together, talking about maths or not. I've known Joe and Jamie since Year 7, so roughly three years, and I have sat next to Joe for all of them. If one of us is stuck or just generally has a problem, we will always help each other. When Jamie joined our table, we became a trio and discussed things together. Is this scary?

This anecdote is taken from Chapter 2 of *Doing Classroom Research: A step-by-step guide for student teachers,* by Sally Elton-Chalcraft et al. (2008).

A question is, therefore, how can purposeful talk be encouraged and developed as a part of a classroom culture?

Paired A/B talk strategy

One approach is to 'label' each student as either an A or a B (which has nothing to do with ability labels) and request that each A and B partnership works together on a question. Working together might, in the first instance, last no more than 2 or 3 minutes; this depends upon the type of question the teacher poses. For example, if the question is 'How many different ways can you think of writing something that means the same as a half?', pairs of pupils might be given 2 minutes to discuss this.

The rationale for using the A/B paired talk strategy in a mathematics classroom is to give students opportunities to rehearse their answers before anyone is asked to provide an answer to the whole class. This, in turn, helps develop students' confidence to provide answers. Another paired task could be: 'Name and draw diagrams of all the different types of triangles (or quadrilaterals) you know of.' Again, students can help each other and I may allocate 2 or 3 minutes to such a task. The intention is to maintain focus on the task (of naming types of quadrilaterals); by setting a time limit, students know the allocated time boundaries for which discussing the task has been given.

Pairs of A/B pairs (envoying information)

This talk strategy is a development of the previous one and is usually described as a process of 'envoying'. The idea is that original A/B pairs discuss answers to a question for a short time, then each B person takes a written record of their discussion to a different A person; this is done by each B person standing up and finding a new A person to talk to. The B person then tells their new A partner what was discussed with the original A partner and the A partner makes a note of what the new B person tells them. After another couple of minutes the original A/B pairs re-form and gather together all the information gained. A typical task could be: 'If the answer is $x = 3$, write some more, different types of equations which are also true.' My intention would be for students to produce answers such as $2x = 6$, $2x + 4 = 10$, $x^2 = 9$, $x^2 + x = 12$, $5x - 2 = 13$ and so on. A follow-up task could be for pairs of students to determine their own 'secret' value of x then produce a set of equations based upon this value, which they give to another pair of students, who then have to try to determine the secret value for x.

Ascertaining students' existing knowledge without requesting 'hands up'

An example which utilizes the A/B talk strategy that I have used many times is to simply hold up a piece of coloured A4 paper and ask students to write down everything they know about what I am holding. After a minute or so I invite individuals to say one thing they have written down. By pooling students' contributions and writing individual responses on the board a potentially interesting list usually emerges. Inevitably responses such as 'It's a piece of paper' and 'It's yellow' usually emerge.

The last time I used this idea, because someone suggested the paper had thickness, another student suggested it must be a cuboid and, therefore, have volume. I was intending to develop the task on this occasion was to consider shapes that can be made from simple folds. However, having ascertained it had a thickness there was potential for a further question: 'Suppose I cut the paper in half and placed the two halves on top of each other, then kept repeating this, how many times would I need to cut it to make the pile higher than the room or higher than Mount Everest?' (The answers, should anyone be interested, are 13 times and 28 times.)

To conclude this chapter I draw upon a quote from Brown et al. (1988: 12):

> People often say 'I teach them but they don't learn'. Well if you know that, stop teaching. Not resign from your job: stop teaching in a way that doesn't reach people.

Gattegno reminds me about how consideration of one's teaching cannot be separated from a consideration of students' learning. In this chapter I have focused on different models for teaching mathematics drawing upon evidence or anecdotes of students' responses to different modes of teaching. By doing this we can see what impact our teaching has. How we gauge effectiveness is important. Engaging in reflective practice and inviting peers to observe and offer feedback upon our teaching, collecting information from various sources, not least of all our students in order to gauge effectiveness is important; far more so than effectiveness being determined by an outsider to the school, such as an inspector or a local authority advisor.

Assessment as an integral part of teaching and learning mathematics

Assessment is an integral part of effective teaching and learning. It allows progress to be recognised and celebrated and it informs the next steps and priorities of both teachers and learners. It is inextricably linked to the curriculum, which provides the content and context of assessment.

This quote from the Qualifications and Curriculum Authority (QCA) in relation to the new National Curriculum (2007) provides a positive viewpoint of assessment. In this chapter I develop this view of assessment, as well as looking at the issue of 'teaching to the test' (T_4) and the potential consequences of T_4 on teaching and learning mathematics.

The most valid and useful types of formative assessment are those which:

- occur during lessons and are a natural part of the many interactions that take place between students and teachers
- inform the learner about their achievements
- help the teacher decide what level of support a pupil or a group of pupils may require at different points in a lesson
- help the learner decide where to go next with a problem or a task.

These four points describe dynamic modes of assessment that take place in classrooms; events occur, information is gathered and processed, and somebody does something with that information for the greater good of those involved. There is, however, a further stage in the formative assessment process. This relates to what any teacher does with information they gather during a lesson and how the teacher uses such information to plan ideas and inputs for future lessons with a group. This is both evaluatory and evolutionary by nature; both being vital aspects of ongoing planning for teaching.

Assessment and classroom practice

Just how the points above translate into classroom practice and what they look like during the 'busyness' of a lesson will largely depend upon the way a teacher operates in the classroom, as well as the ways pupils expect to work. Indeed, the expectations pupils develop about what it means to 'do' or to 'learn' mathematics in any teacher's classroom are vitally important in relation to the way they experience, make sense of and come to view mathematics as a subject per se. The central issue in this chapter, therefore, is how approaches to assessment are connected to classroom culture.

One of the dangers of assessment is the way in which the word becomes a distinct category or as a box to be filled in on lesson planning pro forma sheets. I use the word 'danger' because assessment is something that relates to individuals and how they respond to stimuli and tasks they are presented with. It would be impossible to gather assessment information on every individual in every lesson; at best a teacher might gather information on a handful of individuals in terms of what they have understood and what they might need to do next. Most of this information will be gathered as an outcome of an observation of something a pupil has done and/or in the light of a conversation between a teacher and a pupil. If time allows after a lesson, the teacher may make a brief written note about some pupils' progress. However, in reality there is the next lesson to teach or the next event to attend; dozens of which could easily be listed. In the main any assessments a teacher makes in relation to any pupils reside in a teacher's head; one of the most useful purposes in the way such information is used to inform a teacher's planning for the next lesson.

Before theorizing any further, however, I am going to consider typical or potential types of assessment that could occur during such a module, as well as suggesting some ways of working on summative assessment. To try to do this I am going to look at a set of stimuli forming a module of work on 'coordinates and straight line graphs'. I am going to consider three starting points which I describe as:

1. graphing multiples
2. graphing number bonds
3. four in a line.

These ideas could be used with older KS1 or younger KS2 pupils and, with regard to certain adaptations for task 3, can be developed into AS level mathematics. As such they are suitable for pupils with both wide-ranging potential attainments and for pupils at different stages in their conceptual development.

Graphing multiples

From an early age children are expected to 'learn their times tables' or, mathematically speaking, sets of multiples. How young children experience the learning of their 'tables' and how they experience any assessment of what they have learned is likely to have a significant impact upon their whole view of mathematics, especially upon pupils' self-confidence as learners of mathematics. For this reason I urge caution in this venture. Indeed, I would hope that learning sets of multiples could be viewed as an adventure, as an exploration. I take up the adventure at the time pupils are becoming knowledgeable of mathematical pictures or graphs. More formally graphs are drawn by applying the system of coordinates, which is where the notion of 'graphing multiples' can come to the fore. I shall start the adventure, however, with the use of Cuisenaire rods and a pair of axes.

The idea is to construct a picture by placing different numbers of red Cuisenaire rods in the shape of a staircase:

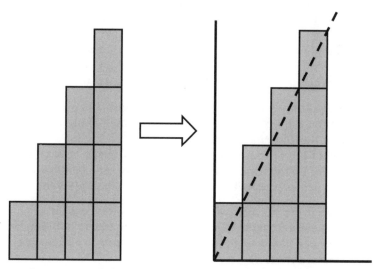

The axes, together with the dotted line on the right-hand side picture, have been added to demonstrate how the left-hand side staircase picture can be turned into a graph. By exploring staircases using green (length 3) rods and pink (length 4) rods, children can look for similarities and differences in the pictures created. A more formal, graphical, representation of multiples of 2 will be appropriate for older children and I develop this below. For now, graphing multiples is about translating information such as:

$$0 \times 2 = 0$$
$$1 \times 2 = 2$$
$$2 \times 2 = 4$$
$$3 \times 2 = 6$$
$$4 \times 2 = 8$$

into a graphical representation via the creation of coordinate pairs as follows. In each calculation we have three pieces of information. The first is the 'start' number, which varies (1, 2, 3 and so on). The second is the multiple or the function ($\times 2$), which is constant. The third is the 'answer', which is always twice the start number. This may seem obvious but, remember, what is obvious to us as adults is not always obvious to children. The important point is to enable pupils to create a picture of what the 'two-times table' can look like by turning the above information into coordinate pairs, that is:

Start	Function	Answer	Coordinates
0	×2	0	(0, 0)
1	×2	2	(1, 2)
2	×2	4	(2, 4)
3	×2	6	(3, 6)
4	×2	8	(4, 8)

By subsequently graphing these sets of coordinates we create a graph of the multiples of 2, which is the same picture as above, excluding the Cuisenaire staircase:

So, what kind of assessment information might anyone gain from setting up this kind of activity in a classroom? I envisage the following achievements have the potential to be observed:

- how pupils use Cuisenaire rods to create staircase designs.
- how pupils compare staircases with different sizes of rods. For example, how does a two-rod staircase compare to a three- or a four-rod staircase?
- whether pupils understand that 0 (zero) multiplied by anything is always zero.

- how pupils produce lists of multiples for x2, x3 and so on.
- whether pupils understand how to convert each list of multiples into sets of coordinate pairs.
- whether pupils can graph these multiples and recognize that each list forms a straight line.
- By graphing more than one set of multiples on the same pair of axes, whether pupils recognize how lines have different degrees of steepness.

Essentially a graph is a generalized picture and, as I have frequently mentioned, generality is fundamentally what mathematics is about. Once any pupil demonstrates their mathematical expertise of drawing graphs of multiples they are only a small step away from drawing graphs of combined functions, such as multiples of 2 plus 1 (or $\times 2 + 1$) and so on. When a pupil can formalize a description such as $\times 2 + 1$ in terms of the graph $y = 2x + 1$ will, of course, be different for different pupils. The key issue here is, when such mathematical behaviour is observed in a pupil (or in a group of pupils), the teacher 'assesses' a readiness for pupils to take a step into more abstract mathematics.

Graphing number bonds

The next idea in my notional module is based upon turning number bonds to 10 into coordinate pairs, that is $1 + 9$, $2 + 8$, $3 + 7$ and so on, and how these pairs can be represented by the coordinate pairs, that is (1, 9), (2, 8), (3, 7) and so on. By graphing these coordinate pairs we obviously produce 'different' graphs to those produced by graphing multiples. The graph of number bonds to 10 also appears in Chapter 9, arising from the 'straws' problem. What I am interested in here are the assessment possibilities a teacher might make in order to determine when it might be appropriate to suggest further tasks. If this task, however, were to follow on from the task of graphing multiples, one key aspect I would be aiming for pupils to recognize is how number bond graphs slope in different directions from graphs of multiples.

Another aspect I would also be looking for in pupils' understanding is how number bonds to 10 and number bonds to any other constant value produce graphs that are parallel to one another. Coming to understand that graphs such as these have a negative gradient will be appropriate for KS3 and KS4 students. However, such a development might be appropriate for more confident KS2 pupils. At the very least, there will be an opportunity for pupils to become aware that graphs that slope 'upwards' from left to right have a positive slope and graphs that slope 'downwards' from left to right are described as having a negative slope.

A further extension to graphing number bonds, in KS3, is to find pairs of values such that when the first value is doubled and the second value is added to it the answer is always a constant. For example, if the constant is 10, then values that would fit the above description would be (0, 10), (1, 8), (2, 6), (3, 4) and so on. These points would produce the graph $2x + y = 10$, or in terms of y, this would be $y = 10 - 2x$. Developments of this situation, therefore, will produce graphs that have negative gradients and different slopes. When students recognize the condition under which some of the graphs they draw are parallel to one another and can explain why this occurs, the teacher must clearly be able to make important assessments and use such information to determine when to move this/these student/s onto a further level of conceptual development. For this module, such a development would be to explore the 'four in a line' problem.

Four in a line

This, ideally, is a game played with two sets of coloured pegs and a pegboard involving two players, each having ten or a dozen pegs of their colour. I say 'ideally' because the game could be played on square grid paper with two different coloured pens. However, while the latter version might be considered less risky, as a consequence of not introducing equipment into the classroom, the former version provides a more tactile, kinesthetic experience. Perhaps the 'best' way might be to use the strategy of letting students decide whether or not to use the equipment in order to play the game. In this way students are more actively involved in a decision-making process.

To make the game even more interesting try using a pegboard that has at least 13 by 13 numbers of holes on it; this is in order for lines with a wider variety of slopes to be produced; a point I return to later. The idea is for students to take turns to place a peg in the board with the intention of producing a continuous or an equally spaced line with four pegs made from the same colour. Once such a situation is achieved the winning line is recorded as a set of coordinates and for this purpose a grid may need to be chalked onto the pegboard. As a starting point I suggest the origin is placed at the bottom left-hand corner. The beauty of this activity is that, depending upon the assessments a teacher may make about what any students might be ready to try out, the origin could be placed more towards the middle of the pegboard, thus enabling students to work with coordinates with negative values and straight lines in all four quadrants.

Once the four coordinate pairs describing a winning line have been recorded, the next task is for students to try to work out the equation of the line that passes through these points. In the first instance the lines are likely to be drawn horizontally or vertically, that is lines of the form $y = c$ (where c is a constant) or $x = c$ or sloping at 45° in a positive or a negative direction, that is lines of the form $y = \pm x \pm c$. One of the more amusing events, when I have used this idea, is to play a game when I place the pegs at a gradient other than horizontally, vertically or $\pm$ 45°. It is always great fun when students exclaim that I am 'cheating' because I appear to have changed the rules, which of course I haven't; I have merely extended them beyond what most students might initially conceive the rules to be. Engaging students with as wide a range of equations of lines that can be drawn within the scope of the size of the pegboard is an important part of the task. One way the idea might be used is for students to write their sets of winning coordinates on strips of sugar paper using felt pens. These winning sets of coordinates can then be placed around the classroom walls (and labelled A, B, C and so on) with the intention for students to work out the equations of the lines so formed. This is a good example of an 'instant' display, where students' own information is used as a resource for practise and consolidation.

Returning to assessment, because the task can be worked on by different students at different rates, there will exist ample opportunities for the teacher to observe students' achievements. By asking students to write about what they have been doing and to give examples of sets of coordinates and the corresponding equations, the outcome of such a written task will provide further information about students' achievements.

At the beginning of this idea I stated there can be opportunities to develop the work into AS level mathematics. To do this, try the following idea. Take a straight line made by four pegs on a pegboard, preferably one that has a gradient other than 0, 8, 1 or -1 and does not pass through the origin. Now rotate the pegboard 90° anticlockwise (say about the centre of the board). What is the equation of this line and how does it compare to the equation of the original line? Now rotate a further 90° anticlockwise (thus having rotated 180° from the original). What is the equation now? What happened for a third 90° rotation? Returning to the original line (and this is where a further powerful attribute of the pegboard comes into its own), what happens when the board is reflected in different axes, $y = 0$, $x = 0$, $y = x$ and $y = -x$? Because the pegs can be seen from the reverse side, the four winning pegs can still be seen and the equations for each of these further seven lines, making eight in all when the original is included, can be calculated.

The beauty of this idea lies in its absolute simplicity, merely taking a pegboard with four pegs in and physically rotating or reflecting the board over. The mathematics, however, is far from simple and once each of these basic transformations have been worked on the teacher might suggest the students consider how they can generalize for m and c for any line $y = mx + c$ for different rotations and reflections. A further development would be for students to consider combinations of transformations, for example, what happens when the line is rotated anticlockwise through 270° then reflected in $x = 0$? At this point we are only a gnat's crotchet away from doing some work on group theory; this, however, is a long way away from the initial concepts that the earlier tasks were initially aimed at (upper KS1/lower KS2 pupils).

At each stage of students' engagement with the ideas described above, there will be plenty of opportunities for a teacher to assess achievement; planning for such opportunities both long term within a scheme of work and short term, lesson by lesson, is an integral part of the process of teaching and learning. Such planning is aimed at students making sense of underlying mathematical systems and the axioms or principles upon which any system is formulated.

All of this, however, may appear to be a long way from the reality of what all teachers and their students have to engage with, which is the testing regime. The biggest issue here, however, is how much direct teaching needs to be carried out in order to prepare students for a test and I develop this issue below.

Teaching to the test

Pupils often 'taught to the test' on post-14 mathematics courses.

The above statement is certainly nothing of a surprise and many teachers, some educational correspondents and certainly this author would have little difficulty in agreeing with it. What may be somewhat surprising is that the notion appears in Ofsted publications from 2006 and 2008. An extract from the 2006 report continues:

> *A narrow focus on meeting examination requirements by 'teaching to the test', so that although students are able to pass the examinations they are not able to apply their knowledge independently to new contexts, and they are not well prepared for further study.*

An extract from the 2008 publication reads:

> *Evidence suggests that strategies to improve test and examination performance, including 'booster' lessons, revision classes and extensive intervention, coupled with a heavy emphasis on 'teaching to the test', succeed in preparing pupils to gain the qualifications but are not equipping them well enough mathematically for their futures. It is of vital importance to shift from a narrow emphasis on disparate skills towards a focus on pupils' mathematical understanding.*

The focus here is on pupils' understanding mathematics and how this is more valuable than merely memorizing methods and carrying out routines. However, while fluency is undeniably a core aspect of learning mathematics, as well as a fundamental process of thinking mathematically, finding a balance between understanding processes and being able to carry out routines with fluency must be carefully considered.

Given that the current system of gauging schools' effectiveness is based upon test results, it is not surprising that much of what drives teaching approaches in mathematics classrooms is a focus on teaching to the test (T_4). It may be useful, therefore, to look at the underlying causes that drive the teaching of mathematics down the road of T_4. The root of T_4 must relate to the pressure teachers feel to get their students to pass tests. Logically, passing a test is achieved by students practising test questions, so they know what to expect and what style of answers they need to produce in order to be 'successful'. In which case why not engage in T_4? Why not play the game?

Below is a cause and effect diagram which, though far from ground-breaking, is intended to try to make sense of the inevitability of why T_4 happens.

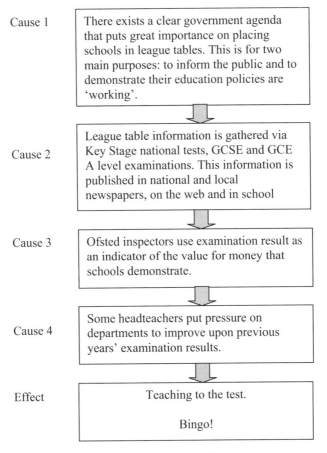

Cause 1 — There exists a clear government agenda that puts great importance on placing schools in league tables. This is for two main purposes: to inform the public and to demonstrate their education policies are 'working'.

Cause 2 — League table information is gathered via Key Stage national tests, GCSE and GCE A level examinations. This information is published in national and local newspapers, on the web and in school

Cause 3 — Ofsted inspectors use examination result as an indicator of the value for money that schools demonstrate.

Cause 4 — Some headteachers put pressure on departments to improve upon previous years' examination results.

Effect — Teaching to the test.

Bingo!

OK, let's stick with the obvious for a while. The government and its inspection regime cannot have it both ways. Seeking to encourage important qualities such as more practical work, more group-work, more discussion, more exploration, more problem solving and more creativity in classrooms requires not only a high degree of risk taking, it also requires a wider variety of assessment methodologies to be recognized. While ever the vehicle for measuring students' levels of achievement is reduced to a timed, written test, carried out in isolation, then all these important qualities or ways of working are not going to be encouraged. Quite simply this is because timed, written tests taken by students, working individually and in silence, cannot possibly measure these fundamentally important qualities and ways of working and learning mathematics, which I think are worth repeating:

- practical work
- collaboration
- discussion
- exploration
- problem solving
- creativity.

For good measure I would also throw in:

- pupil autonomy
- positive mathematical attitude (that is, a capability to function mathematically).

So, no matter how much hand wringing takes place over the dearth of *practical or group-work* (in order) *to stimulate discussion*, teachers will, understandably not be prepared to take the risks or leaps of faith that will be required to work in such ways. The complexity for the government is further compounded by current debates about changes to the post-14 examination system, as discussed by Ashley, *Guardian* (29 October 2007). In her article 'This is what renewal means: turning geese into swans', which is largely about replacing the current GCSE and GCE A level examinations by a system of diplomas, Ashley offers the following:

> It's hard to think of a question more basic than how we measure value in young people... But to a remarkable degree, the way teenagers are graded at school will shape their later careers ... More than that, it shapes the success of the country. When Ed Balls, the schools secretary, asked James Reed, of Reed employment, what he looked for, the answer came back: people who can work in teams, communicate verbally, take risks and make decisions. And what does the current education system throw up? People who work alone, communicate on paper, are risk averse and prefer to look at last year's exam paper.

Perhaps things are changing, even though the change is painstakingly slow. Perhaps, just perhaps we are moving away from a national/political obsession with testing and moving towards the assessment of, and subsequently the development of, far more important and useful skills that industry calls for and will serve the greater good of any country: communication, risk taking, decision making, problem solving, flexibility of mind. Such skills, therefore, need to become the kind of attributes any country's youth are encouraged to develop for their personal advancement as well as their employability in the twenty-first century.

Assessing pupil progress: twenty-first century developments in assessment

In 2006 a pilot teacher assessment scheme was developed across a large number of primary schools. This scheme was initially called 'Monitoring Children's Progress', (MCP) and latterly titled 'Assessing Pupils' Progress' (APP) to bring it in line with a parallel development for assessing secondary students' mathematical achievements.

The relevance of APP on the wider teaching community cannot be understated. This is because as the success of the pilot schemes are recognized both locally and disseminated nationally, the approach used by APP has the potential for impacting upon every teacher.

APP is aimed at developing teacher assessment that does not depend upon scores from tests. The assessment criteria is a set of statements taken from the National Curriculum and supported with 'typically they' statements, to exemplify the kind of information teachers might look for and draw upon when observing the work their pupils produce; this is in order to make assessments against the criteria. Exemplar materials, of children's work demonstrating engagement in mathematics at different levels, have also been produced and referred to as the 'standards files'.

Underpinning teachers' development to use and apply APP in their classrooms is a sense of increasing confidence to make reliable and valid professional judgements. These judgements are based upon the ongoing work a sample group of children produce. This is usually six children per class who represent the range of attainment in the class and are subsequently used as 'benchmarks' for all the pupils in the class. Beyond the use of National Curriculum criteria there is a further collection of unspecified criteria or ways of working that become of paramount importance as teachers engage with the processes of teaching and assessing. These criteria are based upon:

- Children showing evidence of independent thought and action. This was in contrast to children merely mimicking or repeating a method for solving a problem recently given to them by their teacher.
- Seeking to assess Ma1 simultaneously with the other attainment targets (Ma2, Ma3 and Ma4).

- Assessment of mathematical achievement need not only arise in a mathematics lesson. This provided teachers with a framework for utilizing more cross-curricular contexts and looking for evidence of mathematical achievement therein.
- Not all assessments need to be a written record by a pupil to support or justify an assessment. For example, a child might explain something to their teacher or a classroom assistant or another pupil (which the teacher happens to hear); a brief note by the teacher of this event would constitute sufficient evidence.

As with a GCSE project (which I describe below), this project had massive curriculum development outcomes for the pilot schools involved. As an external moderator for APP, I had many first-hand conversations with teachers who remarked how valuable the APP framework was, not only in terms of making assessments but also as a guide for curriculum coverage and for curriculum development. As such APP had a significant impact upon teachers carrying out more coherent, joined-up lesson planning, which in some cases eschewed the orthodoxy of teaching in a three-part lesson style; teachers recognizing the opportunities for the emergence and value of developing 'continuation' type lessons.

APP, therefore, brings together the key issues of planning for teaching and teaching, learning and assessment and, as such, meets the central issues of the quote at the beginning of this chapter from the QCA:

> Assessment is an integral part of effective teaching and learning. It allows progress to be recognised and celebrated and it informs the next steps and priorities of both teachers and learners. It is inextricably linked to the curriculum, which provides the content and context of assessment.

Trying to separate out the act of assessment from planning, teaching and learning is a falsehood. The way any teacher engages in their professional development is through the control they have over deciding upon how to weave each of these elements into their practice. Professional development is much more than attending a course and applying the ideas presented; it is about personal autonomy and the ways teachers are encouraged to take responsibility for their development. To remove the fundamental element of assessment from teachers' professionality, through the imposition of a testing regime, is flawed thinking.

The great value of APP, therefore, is that it both validates and encourages teacher assessment of pupils' ongoing classwork; this includes seeking opportunities to notice how pupils demonstrate engagement in problem-solving and decision-making processes. Evidence of achievement is neither taken from tests, nor is it taken solely from mathematics contexts but wherever such achievement is recognized across other subject areas. Clearly this is more easily organized in a primary school where the class teacher sees their children operate in a variety of cross-curricular contexts. However, recent developments in secondary schools, through functional skills and through the Bowland Trust initiative, are aimed at learning through more authentic, broader contexts and assessing skills well beyond those that can be assessed in an examination room. For the teacher, at whatever stage they may be at in their career, the APP approach to assessment creates a common framework for a range of developments in professional expertise.

Assessment for the twenty-first century and the Magnificent Seven

The following couple of pages are not intended to be a sentimental journey. My reason for writing about a project which began over 20 years ago and lasted for nine years is because I believe the initiative was at least 30 years ahead of its time; certainly within the domain of teacher assessment in mathematics classrooms. I also believe the approach to assessment that I describe below is wholly consistent with recent assessment QCA APP initiatives and, as such, continues to have relevance as an approach to assessment in the twenty-first century.

The project was a pilot 100 per cent teacher-assessed GCSE scheme, created by some members of the ATM in conjunction with officers at the Southern Examination Group (SEG). This pilot GCSE scheme began in 1986 and ran until 1995. There were seven schools involved hailing from Cumbria (two schools), Manchester, Telford, Oxford (two schools) and Weston-Super-Mare. During the first two years of certification, 1988 and 1989, the 100 per cent model was operated without any terminal examination needing to be taken by students and the whole of the grade was determined via in-school and inter-school moderation. The original criteria for assessment were based upon students' capabilities to demonstrate the skills of: implementation, interpretation, communication, content knowledge, mathematical attitude, autonomy, evaluation, working in groups. For each criterion there was a set of assessment descriptors for grades A, C and E and students' work was measured against these grade descriptors. At in-school and termly inter-school moderation meetings, teachers would bring along portfolios of work which samples of their students had produced.

In the main, schools devised modules of work that tended to run for a minimum of three weeks. Each module was based upon students demonstrating their understanding of the required GCSE curriculum content knowledge, as defined by the then Schools Examinations and Assessment Council (SEAC). Because schools adopted a modular structure, investigative Ma1-type approaches were naturally integrated into the work students produced. Students produced portfolios of work and any piece of work had the potential to be used as part of the final assessment, in terms of the GCSE grade they achieved and were awarded. Final assessment was agreed with an external moderator who looked at a sample of students' work that covered the entire grade range. Because each portfolio that was submitted for final moderation had to demonstrate coverage of the curriculum content this meant a portfolio contained, on average, ten or so different modules of work.

As one might imagine, a massive amount of professional and curriculum development work took place during moderation meetings and this became a notable outcome of the ATM-SEG GCSE scheme. A typical scenario would be as follows: a teacher would read through a portfolio of work of a student from another school, looking to match the assessment criteria against what appears in the portfolio. Invariably the teacher would come across a piece of work that looked 'interesting', something they had not tried themselves in their own teaching. Inevitably, once the business of moderation had been completed, the moderating teacher would ask the class teacher what the stimulus had been that had lead the student to produce the aforementioned piece of work. A conversation would take place, not just between the class teacher and the moderating teacher, but also with other teachers. This was cooperative curriculum development in action; ideas were swapped and taken back to classrooms to be tried out. I remember gaining much professional development through these meetings and through the network of teachers involved. Here are a few typical ideas that, at the time, were new to me:

Averaging and averaging

- Choose three numbers, say 3, 7, 10.
- Find their (mean) average (20/3 or 6.6 recurring).
- Add this value to the list and cross out the first value.
- Now find the average of the new list 7, 10, 20/3 (71/9 or 7.8 recurring).
- Repeat (that is, find the average of 10, 20/3 and 71/9).
- Keep repeating until something happens.

What is the connection between the number that emerges (when something happens) and the original numbers?

Constructing 'right' pyramids 1

Construct a square-based pyramid with its apex perpendicular to one of the corners of the base and with a perpendicular height equal to the length of the base. Make three, join them together (with sticky tape) and see what happens.

Constructing 'right' pyramids 2

Construct a square-based pyramid with its apex perpendicular to the centre of the base and with a perpendicular height equal to half of the length of the base. Make six of these and 'hinge' them together (with sticky tape) and see what happens.

The beginning of the end of the ATM-SEG GCSE

After the seven schools had managed to run a 100 per cent teacher-assessed model without a terminal examination scheme for two years, SEAC got nervous and a group of us were invited to explain our rationale and why we believed a continuation of the 100 per cent coursework weighting was desirable, feasible and in line with national criteria. A statement in the criteria stated that syllabi should 'normally' have a balance of teacher-assessed work and terminal examination; we argued that mathematically speaking a 'normal' distribution included those areas under the extremes of the bell-curve; this had been the same argument that had won favour when the syllabus was originally presented to SEAC, and after all, at the other end of the bell-curve distribution there would be those people who favoured assessment based upon a 100 per cent terminal examination model. However, despite our position we were asked to produce a terminal examination weighted at 50 per cent. The only concession was that half of this weighting could be allocated to a 'process-based' examination, where students were expected to answer just three questions (from a choice of five questions) in one of the examinations. The other 25 per cent was apportioned to a more traditional type of examination paper. Although this approach would now be considered somewhat revolutionary by comparison to the type of questions that appear in current examination papers, for the schools involved it was the best of a bad job.

One of the more interesting features of this GCSE scheme was that cheating was not an issue. This was because teachers became naturally knowledgeable about the work their students produced on a lesson-by-lesson basis. Furthermore, because schools did not entertain the use of 'bolt-on' or prescribed 'one-off' tasks, typical of coursework created by examination boards (and thankfully abandoned by 2007), the ATM-SEG scheme had a built-in assessment integrity; this naturally supported teacher autonomy and professionalism in terms of creating tasks and modules for assessment that supported students' learning. This was assessment *for* learning and assessment *of* learning in action.

In this chapter I have attempted to draw together the issues of teaching, learning, assessment and professional development. I argue that each of these elements are interlinked and in fact cannot and should not be separated from one another. A key issue is how much and what kind of information needs to be collected and recorded. Clearly if a teacher spends too much time recording assessments, this will reduce the amount of time available for planning interesting lessons, and thus a balance must be struck. Ultimately teachers will come to know far more about their students' achievements than can be ascertained by timed written tests. What is important is that teachers' judgements are valued and trusted by stakeholders beyond the immediate life of any classroom. This leads to a focus upon tasks offered to students and what kind of opportunities might exist for teacher assessment. I have discussed two complimentary models of assessment, APP (which has been developed since 2006) and the ATM-SEG GCSE (which began in 1985). Both models were aimed at strengthening teachers' professionality in terms of trusting judgements they might make in contrast to 'trusting' the scores students might gain from centrally imposed tests.

Working with teaching assistants $\boxed{8}$

My impression of the teaching assistants (TAs) I have had the pleasure to work with is that they are admirable educationalists. This is borne out for me by both classroom experience, limited though that may be in the past few years, and more so in the context of continuing professional development courses that I have the privilege to construct and teach. From my overall and generalized experience of working with TAs (in the region of a hundred), they are down-to-earth people who have pupils' best interests at heart and have an enormous amount to offer the pupils and the teachers they support. This grounded way of being has pulled me up short on more than one occasion, as was revealed in one of the mathematics courses I led. I had been offering a range of puzzles and problems and glibly said to a group: 'You can try some of these puzzles in your spare time at home'. However, before I could take breath one of the group, Jane, responded: 'Spare time ... what's that? Just remember, Mike, you're talking to a room full of women!'

This rates as my best ever put-down; fortunately it was meant as an amusing riposte to an ill thought-out comment I had made (well, given it was said by a Scouser and an Evertonian at that, I am sure it was intended as amusing).

One role teaching assistants play, though certainly not a role they set out to take on, is the proverbial 'fly on the wall' in other teachers' classrooms. As such, they gain fascinating insights into teachers' practices, some of which will be about observing skilled professionals at work. Other insights, however, may occasionally be of a less positive nature. My evidence for these last two statements is in the form of short pieces of writing, freely and anonymously supplied to me when I have asked course delegates to write a few words about when they feel to be at their most effective in classrooms. I have used some of their responses in this book. At this juncture, from an ethical perspective, I should explain that delegates knew in advance they were only to provide me with responses in the knowledge that I may use some of them in writing such as this. The questions I posed were:

- Under what circumstances do you feel to be most effective in the work you do?
- Can you give one or two examples of issues or ideas that you think you will embrace in your teaching as a result of this course?

This chapter, therefore, is based upon issues relating to working with teaching assistants (TAs). I look at typical activities we have tried out on five-day primary and secondary mathematics subject knowledge courses, which I had the privilege to teach. I explore some learning issues for pupils as well as discussing what it is like to work as a TA from their perspective; the information for this is taken from those pieces of writing. I also consider planning-for-teaching issues, pupil-learning issues, depth versus acceleration, organizational and pedagogic issues.

Working with TAs proved to be a fascinating experience, mainly because those I have worked with have a wide range of experience in different schools, across Key Stages from Foundation to KS4. I have learned a lot by teaching these courses, which were based upon the following aims:

- To develop TAs own mathematical thinking and subject knowledge.
- To consider how ideas might be adapted and used in classrooms.
- To consider the nature of children's learning of mathematics and how best we can support this development.

During the CPD courses, as I reveal later in this chapter, we worked on a wide range of mathematical tasks, puzzles and problems and spent time considering their responses, mathematically speaking, to the ideas, as well as discussing how the tasks might be used within their own work situations.

Diversity, responsibility and support

A key issue to arise from my work with TAs has been to find out about the diverse skills TAs have, the types of duties they can be asked to carry out and the responsibilities that can be bestowed upon them. Some TAs, for example, are able to take greater ownership for the work they do and this is because of the way they are entrusted to try out their own ideas, with individuals, small groups and even whole classes. At the other end of this scale, some TAs found themselves in situations where they were not provided with any information about the lesson they were due to give support in and instead had to sort out what the class teacher was teaching and react accordingly. There are issues of trust here, about recognizing capability, as well as the class teacher becoming sufficiently confident to entrust another adult who has different skills and different relationships with students. Therefore, to be able to 'let go' and cede responsibility to the other adult is a key factor in the teacher-TA professional relationship.

Of course, how a professional relationship is constructed is tenuous and often delicate; yet clearly important with regard to developing a harmonious working relationship as the following comment suggests:

> ● If teaching pupils away from the class, I like to be given a structure to work within and not just left to 'sink or swim'. To have a good relationship with the class teacher I want to be able to ask for help also.

This comment leads me to my next section, planning for teaching.

Planning for teaching

Most of the TAs attending the CPD courses said they have excellent working relationships with classroom teachers and the following two comments are symptomatic of this:

> ● In my school I discuss with the teachers the work I do and the best use of my time. We also discuss the effects and any need for change.
> ● From the rapport I have with all members of staff I know the work I do is appreciated. We chat, we listen, we undertake to work together. We are friends and colleagues and socialize outside school.

In such circumstances pupils are clearly going to get the best from a TA and this is because the TA feels valued and included. One of the more complex tasks for teachers and therefore for TAs is getting information in advance of a lesson on what the lesson is about and what role the teacher would like the TA to play. Realistically for a classroom teacher to be able to make their lesson plans week by whole week is difficult and in some cases impossible. This is because classrooms are unpredictable places and what happens in one lesson impacts upon and influences the planning for a subsequent lesson. The following comment about the conditions when one TA felt to be least effective, therefore, is one that requires some analysis:

> • I am least effective when I have not been given lesson plans. This year I have seen none. I would like to know what maths knowledge is required before the lesson, preferably the week before.

There are clearly complex issues here about how any class teacher is able to 'find the time' to communicate with a TA prior to the lesson. The reality is that schools are incredibly busy places and, to reiterate, planning a week's worth of lessons in advance is not always feasible. Neither, however, is it necessarily desirable and this is because lesson plans rarely (ever?) run to plan and teachers inevitably find themselves having to plan a subsequent lesson as a direct consequence of what happened in the previous lesson.

I cannot offer any easy solutions to the difficulties of keeping a TA regularly informed or updated about the specific content of the 'next' lesson and the role the teacher would most want them to play. The most effective ways that teachers and TAs work together is based upon the professional relationships they develop and the trust they build up between one other. Having said all of this, there is one key, essential way that TAs can become more confident about the roles they play in mathematics classrooms and this is to provide them with opportunities to engage in mathematical thinking; this is a responsibility for headteachers and local authorities as well as other departments.

Developing confidence and developing competence

A central issue to emerge, therefore, from the CPD courses, related to how or whether TAs were empowered in their schools to try out the ideas and use the kind of resources we explored. One of the more exciting outcomes was the recognition that, as they developed a greater range of ideas and strategies for use in the classroom, the greater confidence they felt to become more proactive in the classroom. This is in contrast to carrying out reactive roles where some TAs feel their job is to reinterpret a class teacher's explanation to those pupils they have responsibility for supporting.

Two reasons for this increase in confidence was due to the nature of the courses which:

1. Provided opportunities for TAs to work on mathematical tasks and problems and develop their mathematical thinking.
2. Sought to increase pedagogic awareness of the value of making greater use of investigative approaches and practical resources in their teaching. As such all ideas used on the courses were either of a practical or an investigative nature; many requiring the use of equipment such as:
   - dice
   - dominoes
   - counters
   - clocks
   - cards
   - straws
   - ATM mats
   - paper, for the folding thereof
   - Cuisenaire rods
   - square nine-pin geoboards and elastic bands
   - 100-square grids
   - place value grids.

We also carried out some visualization and some 'people-maths' problems. My intention was to make the mathematics 'hands on', exploratory, accessible, achievable and, therefore, enjoyable; competence breeds confidence and confidence breeds competence. Below are descriptions of a small subset of the many ideas we worked on; first though I offer my rationale for using resources such as cards, dice and so on.

Rationale for using cards, dice, dominoes, counters, cubes and any other practical equipment

One way we make sense of anything is through kinesthetic, 'hands-on' experiences. In the mathematics classroom, such experiences might be gained by working with equipment or being involved in a people-maths type task. I define a hands-on experience as something that causes engagement in the action, by comparison to being either observers of any action or viewers of a teacher's actions. Through hands-on experience pupils can literally get hold of a concrete resource and through their engagement with the resource make sense of the underlying mathematics and slowly move towards more abstract under- standings. Working with a resource, such as a set of playing cards, some dice, a set of dominoes or some linking cubes means, at the very least, they have something to count; something they are holding in their hands. Using such resources allows pupils to hold them, move them around, match them together or build something; this provides a different learning experience to looking at an illustration in a textbook or a picture downloaded onto an interactive whiteboard. The act of pupils getting hold of a resource and seeing what they can do with it puts them more in control of their learning and fosters opportunities to think and to work creatively. Below I suggest some specific tasks that cards, dominoes and counters might be used for.

Playing cards

Playing card games inherently provides opportunities for arithmetic and strategic ways of thinking. Cribbage is an excellent example, and a two-person version, for there are many different versions according to regional location, is played as follows: The dealer deals six cards each and both players have to place two cards, face down, into the 'box'; this is an extra 'hand' which players take turns to have according to who deals. The idea is to score points according to the following situations:

- Any two cards that add up to 15 scores two points (the court cards take a face value of 10).
- Any run of three cards (for example 6, 7, 8) of any suit scores three points; a run of four scores four points (some people count a run of four as two overlapping runs of three).

- Two cards of the same face value (a pair) scores two points (so three cards of the same face value scores six points).
- One can also score with a 'flush', all four cards of the same suit. However, some people insist that a 'flush in the box' must also include the card turned over, but we have not got to that rule so far, so you will need to read on for further clarification.

Once each player has put their two cards in the box, the non-dealer cuts the remaining pack and the dealer turns over the next card. If a jack is turned over the dealer scores two points (accompanied by the phrase 'two for doing it'). A feature of cribbage is the little sayings and 'ditties', which is all part of the 'language' of cribbage.

The next phase of the game now begins. This is when players take turns to place their cards down in front of themselves so that the face values of each card played is accumulated until a maximum of 31 is gained. Whoever plays a card so a running total of 31 exactly is made scores two points. Whoever plays the last card in any running total up to 31, but cannot make 31 exactly, scores just one point. Once all eight cards have been played, players gather up their own four cards and score their hand as above, adding the card earlier cut and turned over as the fifth card. The dealer also scores the box hand. Cribbage is usually scored on a 'crib' board, which traditionally is a wooden board with four sets of 30 holes in, and the winning total is 121 (or 'twice round'). In the classroom, pupils can keep a record of their scores and it might be useful just to play up to 61.

Games such as cribbage, therefore, involve lots of counting and the development of strategies linked to what to 'keep' and what to 'put in the box', as well as the order the cards are played prior to 'scoring' each hand. As mentioned above, cribbage has its own language and this certainly enhances the playing of the game. Although all the rules above make it sound a rather complicated game, it is, in actuality, quickly learned and with practise can be played at speed. The game also provides much pleasure.

As well as trying out simple tricks (see *100+ Ideas for Teaching Mathematics* (Ollerton: 2007)) playing cards can also be used for practising:

- Number bonds to 10:
  Using just two suits of cards with the face values from 1 to 9, place these 18 cards face down and play the game of pairs. The idea is for pupils to try to turn over two cards that total to 10. If a pair of cards

is selected that form a number bond to 10, that player keeps them as a pair. If two cards are chosen which do not total to 10, they are turned back over. The game continues by players taking turns. The player with the most number of pairs of cards which each totals to 10 is the winner. At the end of each game pupils might count how many lots of 10s they have found; thus reinforcing the concept of multiples of 10.

An extension of this game is for each player to turn over three cards and pupils then have to choose any pair of cards that total to 10.

- Number bonds to 11.
Place nine cards (from a complete pack) face up in a three by three array. All the number cards take on their face value, so an ace counts as one and so on. If any pair of cards totals up to 11, place two new cards, one on each. Jacks, queens and kings do not have any value. However, if one of each (that is a J, a Q and a K) are turned over you may place a new card on top of each of these three court cards. The idea is to use up all the cards in a pack. At the end, if the patience game has been successfully completed, there should be three pairs of cards that each total to 11, together with one jack, one queen and one king. In my experience, this game of patience is usually successfully completed on approximately one in every three attempts.

Using dominoes

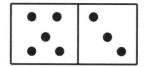

Dominoes are another marvellous resource that can be used to engage pupils in process skills such as ordering, pattern spotting, generalizing and a range of concepts including: counting, adding, multiplying, fractions and coordinates.

Some tasks include:

- How many dominoes are there in a set of dominoes up to 3/3?
- How many dominoes are there in other sets?
- How many spots are there in a set of dominoes up to 3/3?
- How many spots are there in other sets?
- Can you work out answers to the question above without counting all of the spots?

- Remove all the doubles from a double six set and place the remaining 21 dominoes into three sets of seven so the total for each set is the same.
- Turn all 28 dominoes over so they are face down. Players take turns to turn over two dominoes with the intention of adding the spots together in order to make a total of 12. The player with the most pairs at the end is the winner.
- Remove all the dominoes with a blank (this will become clear in a moment). Turn each remaining domino into a fraction, such that the numerator is less than the denominator. Try to place these fractions in order from smallest to largest.
- Take three dominoes and change the numbers into coordinate pairs. Plot these pairs on square grid paper and join them together. What kind of triangles are made?
- Plot the points from the above the 'other way round' and see what happens.

And finally, playing the game of 5s and 3s. This is a brilliant game for helping pupils develop knowledge and fluency with multiples of 5 and multiples of 3. My experience of playing this game in different contexts, in the pub, on CPD courses and at parent/teacher meetings, is that not everyone knows the rules; yes I know this is an unbelievable travesty, but it is nevertheless the case. I shall, therefore, briefly explain how the game is played.

The game of 5s and 3s

In pairs, each player takes nine dominoes and the remaining ten are unused. The game is played like ordinary dominoes, where values that match must be placed next to one another. Pupils take turns to play a domino and the one who goes first can choose any from their 'hand'. The idea is to add together the two 'ends' and the score is determined by how many 5s and/or 3s divide into this total. So, if the domino to be played is the 5-1 then the two ends total to six, which is 2 × 3, so this person scores two points. If the next person plays a 1-4, the two ends now total to nine (5 + 4) and this is a score of three (3 × 3). If a pupil plays a double, this is placed 'vertically', so all the spots on a double are added to whatever the value of the other end happens to be. It is possible to make a total of 15, by having a double five on one end and a five on the other (or a double six and a three); this situation scores eight points because 15 is both five 3s and three 5s.

This game can easily be changed to 5s and 2s or 3s and 4s. I realize this is something of a travesty for traditional domino players. However, adapting the game as a way of engaging pupils in developing fluency with short division and adding is something to be encouraged.

Using counters

The following task is an adaptation of a task described in *Points of Departure* (book 1, idea 12). The original task begins with three counters. However, in order to make it even more accessible, I chose to offer a problem using just two counters in the first instance. The problem goes as follows:

- I have two counters. On the front of the first counter is the number 1. On the front of the second counter is the number 3. We do not know what the numbers are on the back of each of the counter. The different possible totals I can make when I spin the two counters and add together the numbers that land face up are 4, 5, 6 and 7. What could the numbers be on the back of each counter? There are two different solutions to this problem and asking pupils to try to work out both of these may help them gain further insights into the problem.
- Choose your own four numbers and try to generate a list of four consecutive totals. Give your totals to a partner as well as the 'front' two numbers and see if they can work out your other two numbers.
- Repeat for above but just give a partner the four totals and one of the 'front' numbers to see if s/he can work out the other three numbers.
- With three counters, on the front of the first is a 5, on the front of the second is a 6 and on the front of the third is a 7. The possible consecutive totals are 18, 19, 20, 21, 22, 23, 24 and 25. What could the numbers be on the back of each of the three counters? For this problem there are quite a few solutions, but can they all be found?

Learning issues for pupils and the three-part lesson

In the main, though certainly not exclusively so, TAs support pupils who struggle to learn mathematics. As such, TAs see first-hand much of what pupils struggle with in mathematics classrooms and many are able to empathize with such struggles. One of the most insightful comments I received was:

> • Often some children have just made a start when it is time for the plenary.

This comment begs an important issue about pupils having sufficient time to make sense of a concept, practise it and confirm their understanding of it.

The comment also paints an interesting picture of the class teacher being under pressure to organize a lesson plenary, irrespective of whether holding a plenary is strategically purposeful. Perhaps the relatively recent orthodoxy of teaching to a three-part lesson framework continues to hold sway for some teachers in some classrooms; perhaps this orthodoxy is expected to be complied with by some headteachers and some local authority advisors and 'encouraged' or expected through inspection. It is, however, nonsensical to adhere to a three-part lesson framework if such a structure gets in the way of pupils' learning. A three-part lesson might fit a cosy conception of what an effective lesson looks like. However, if some children find themselves being 'plenaried' (I just made up that word) before they have had an opportunity to develop their thinking, because 'it's time for the plenary', then I suggest the three-part lesson framework becomes a prohibitor to effective learning. My concern is that children are being accelerated onwards at the expense of depth of understanding; again there is a government agenda at work here about seeking to demonstrate that 'Persil not only washes whiter but also does it faster'. I believe there is a depth versus acceleration discussion to be engaged with and I develop this below.

Depth versus acceleration

> Much of the mathematical experience of most pupils is extremely fragmented, as they proceed from one small item to another in quick succession. (HMI, 1985: 6)

This quotation is taken from one of the ten objectives for teaching mathematics: in-depth study in mathematics. In part I think this objective is about purposefully slowing learners down instead of speeding them up. How fast anybody understands anything and is able to use, apply and transfer their learning is clearly dependent upon individuals and their different rates of cognition. As such, finding ways of supporting differentiated learning, so learners can develop their thinking to different, appropriate levels to try to ensure consolidation of a learned skill, is central to the work of teachers and teaching assistants.

Solving a range of problems in non-obvious or unfamiliar contexts is at the heart of mathematical activity. Asking pupils to seek patterns and from these to look for generalities underpins the learning of mathematics. A 'good' problem-solving task will simultaneously cause learners to engage in such mathematical thinking and at the same time to practise and consolidate learned skills.

As an example I offer the context of setting up and solving linear equations. The context is based upon some work that I first met via *The South Nottinghamshire Project*, which was originally published in the mid-1970s. The particular idea is one called 'pyramids'.

This idea begins in a beautifully simple way and is about working with any three numbers as set out in the arrangement below. The task is to find out the value at the bottom of the pyramid by using the rule of adding the numbers in the two boxes to give the number in the box immediately below. So, starting with 7, 8 and 4 the answer in the bottom box will be 27. Some questions to arise from this situation might be:

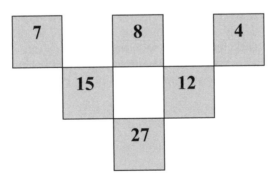

- What different sets of three numbers can be used to generate an answer of 27?
- How are the starting numbers connected with the answer?
- What happens if four numbers are chosen to start with?

Pupils developing their own equations

The problem is to find out the missing value if the total in a box below is found by adding the 'values' in the two boxes above (as before).

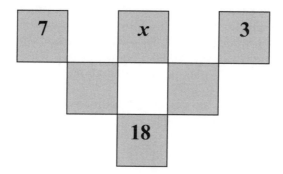

In the first instance this problem could be solved using trial and improvement. The main intention, however, is to use algebra as shown below:

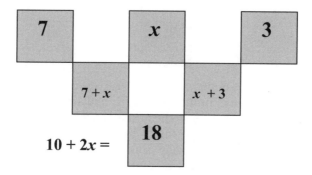

This approach creates an opportunity for pupils to set up the equation in order to solve the problem. Because pupils are setting up equations for each problem they work on, two important aspects of learning come to the fore. The first is about pupils seeing for themselves how algebra can be used to solve a problem. The second is about pupils creating equations themselves and this is quite different from them being presented with a list of equations in an exercise from a textbook where, often without rhyme or reason, they are asked to calculate missing values.

An approach I have found useful for solving 'simple' linear

equations is one often referred to as the 'cover up' method. This involves covering up the unknown quantity of $2x$ and getting pupils to ask themselves the question: 'What else do I need to add on to 10 to make 18?' Clearly the answer is 8 and this leads to **2x** being equal to 8, and **x**, therefore, being equal to 4. Checking the answer is an important part of the process.

Asking pupils to explain what they have understood about an approach or a strategy they have used is a further aspect of the deepening process. An explanation could be: writing about, presenting to peers, making a poster about, explaining to a teaching assistant or to a teacher.

A further deepening task could be to consider subtraction instead of addition, for example:

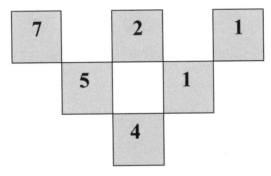

Of course the example above is a nice 'clean' uncomplicated one. However, if the numbers 7, 2, 1 had been written in a different order, say 2, 1, 7, so the answer becomes 7, then pupils are provided with an opportunity to practise computing with negative numbers. Algebraically, this would appear as:

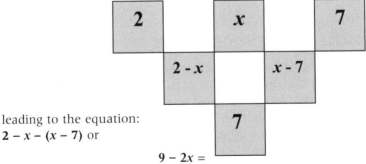

leading to the equation:
$2 - x - (x - 7)$ or
$9 - 2x =$

I have used all the ideas that appear in this chapter in both primary and secondary classrooms and in CPD sessions with teaching assistants. As with all the other ideas in this book, my rationale for using them and writing about them is because they enable learners of all ages and at all stages in their cognitive development to access mathematics and, in doing so, to develop confidence as mathematicians. The key issue is that of developing TAs' mathematical capabilities, in order that they can support pupils and teachers; by developing mathematical competences, TAs will also develop strategies for supporting pupils.

Progression in mathematical concept development

9

Progression is to do with the ways in which teachers and pupils together explore, make sense of and construct pathways through the network of ideas, which is mathematics. Each person's 'map' of the network and of the pathways connecting different mathematical ideas is different, thus people understand mathematics in different ways.

This marvellous quote, from the original National Curriculum *Mathematics Non-statutory Guidance* in 1989, gets to the heart of teaching and learning mathematics. In this chapter I consider this fundamentally important issue of progression in mathematics, in the way tasks can be used to aide progression in teaching and learning mathematics.

One of the key issues about progression is to recognize that mathematical concept development does not happen linearly, nor at the same rate or depth for different pupils. With this in mind I feel the above quote is important because it describes progression in mathematics as a network, about different pupils making sense of or mapping out their understanding of mathematics through the pathways they create. However, this description is at odds with the way school mathematics is presented in step-by-step lists in each version of the curriculum. Fortunately, the latest (2007) version is a far less prescriptive document and offers teachers greater opportunities to be creative in the way they plan and teach mathematics. Indeed, even the logo, as a flowing intertwining set of different coloured ribbons, with each subject being represented by one of the ribbons, creates an impression of an interconnected network; a recognition that learning is neither linear nor straightforward; that the different disciplines have many points of connectivity.

Pennies dropping, progression and learning mathematics

The process of learning mathematics, or even better the process of anyone learning to function mathematically, is certainly not straightforward; this was amusingly demonstrated by a third-year mathematics undergraduate student in the following way. I had been asked to provide two days input into the students' course, to develop ideas for the mathematics school classroom as part of a mathematics education module. We had been working on a problem described in *100+ Ideas for Teaching Mathematics* (2007) about shifts on a 100 grid (idea no 40: 47), about working on an 'extended' 100 grid, as below:

	90	91	92	93	94	95	96	97	98	99	100		
		81	82	83	84	85	86	87	88	89	90		
		71	72	73	74	75	76	77	78	79	80		
		61	62	63	64	65	66	67	68	69	70		
		51	52	53	54	55	56	57	58	59	60	61	
		41	42	43	44	45	46	47	48	49	50		
		31	32	33	34	35	36	37	38	39	40		
		21	22	23	24	25	26	27	28	29	30		
		11	12	13	14	15	16	17	18	19	20		
⁻1	0	1	2	3	4	5	6	7	8	9	10	11	12
⁻11				⁻6									
⁻21													

The idea is for pupils to fill in the missing spaces so they see that the boundary of the original 100 grid is, potentially, infinite and that numbers are repeated and do not hold a single unique place in the extended two-dimensional grid.

Anyway, after a few minutes I heard Emma mutter something, perhaps to herself, though sufficiently audible for me to hear. This utterance seemed to be a comment that she had really understood a basic mathematical structure, so I asked: 'Has a penny just dropped?' Emma replied: 'Yes, but this penny has ended up in the piggy bank and not on the floor'. Two things interested me about this comment: the first was to experience a different interpretation of 'pennies dropping'; the second, more importantly, was the issue that here was someone who had clearly understood, I assumed for the first time, a very basic mathematical notion, by comparison with the level of mathematics she was currently studying on her degree course.

Here was an example therefore of an adult who had made progress in her mathematical development yet was still learning about a fundamental mathematical structure. Emma was clearly progressing towards working at degree level in mathematics but had only just fully understood a concept that would have first been introduced to her as a 12 or 13 year old. Of course, there is a difference between being able to accurately carry out a mathematical computation and gaining a fundamental understanding of the concept involved; but understanding must surely be the most important aspect of learning mathematics. Perhaps this gap between being able to 'do' mathematics and understanding mathematics is a by-product of our system of measuring achievement.

Without certain concepts being in place, it is difficult, though certainly not impossible, to learn higher-order concepts. For example, learning about the way counting numbers are organized would seem to be a necessary precursor to calculating with those numbers. However, because mathematics is fundamentally about pattern, variance, invariance and, therefore, generality, we do not need to get pupils to count all the way to, say, a thousand in order to appreciate that the next whole number after 1000 is 1001. Likewise, by knowing $3 + 5 = 8$ pupils can generalize that $30 + 50 = 80$ and $300 + 500 = 800$ (or $3x + 5x = 8x$).

Indeed, one could argue that to keep returning a pupil to something they have failed to grasp, for whatever reason, can act as a demotivator and at worst cause a learner to become more deeply stuck. This is clearly demonstrated when, for example, Year 10 or Year 11 students seemingly 'fail' to make sense of a concept they initially met at primary school.

On 'stuckness' and pennies not dropping

I am sure others will recognize scenarios such as 15 and 16 year olds who are classified as 'low ability' who are not able to carry out seemingly simple computations such as 514 take 267 or 34 multiplied by 27 or how to calculate 10 per cent of £15. However, one could argue that the reason for such events occurring may be as a result of students being bored or frustrated at having to do the same kind of work which they associate with what they did, or more likely could not do, seven or eight years previously. The rationale, I assume, for asking 'low-ability' students to revisit past failures is a sense that they cannot proceed with higher-order concepts until all the foundations are firmly in place.

A significant problem arises, therefore, when a child has got 'stuck' with a particular basic concept and it appears the child is unable to progress further. My concern, having lived through such an event, is that it is not always the child who is stuck but rather the teacher, by not having a range of methods, strategies or resources to help the child overcome their 'stuckness'.

The event I refer to above took place over 25 years ago and was about one of my own children's stuckness with reading between ages six and seven. I remember him coming home with the Ladybird, *Peter and Jane* reading scheme, first book 1a, then 1b, next book 2a, then 2b, then 3a followed by 3b, then 3a, then 3b. No, I have not made a typing error here, I do mean 3a then 3b, then book 3a followed by... yes you've guessed it... 3b! Well he certainly was stuck, seemingly unable to proceed beyond book 3b.

As it happened he was to soon start at a new school (though for entirely different reasons and not because I had lost faith in his teacher's ability to help him learn to read). I explained the situation to his new teacher and she said she would assess him and, if necessary, work with him in a small non-readers' group. Here they used 'flash' cards, had fun and played lots of word association games. One day, about four weeks later he came home in tears; his teacher had said he could no longer stay in his small group. This was because he was answering the questions too quickly; he was, she assessed, ready to read and, therefore, could now learn to read in the whole class. Eighteen months later he completed reading *Lord of the Rings* entirely of his own volition.

There is, in my opinion, a 100 per cent direct comparison between learning the basics of reading and the basics of understanding mathematics; they are after all language and vocabulary dependent. The premises that underpin learning are connected to providing learners with tasks that:

- pupils can do
- pupils see value in doing or recognize a need to do
- pupils enjoy doing (I define enjoyment as gaining either mental or physical fulfilment)
- pupils can achieve success through and gain confidence in doing
- challenge learners to extend what they can already do.

This final point is about moving learners outside a comfort zone; all too often we hear the phrase 'pupils working at their own level'. However, effective learning takes place when pupils learn to move beyond their current level of understanding.

One aspect of the craft of a teacher is to find different ways of working on pupils' cognitive development and this is what my son's teacher, at his new school was able to do. She did what all effective teachers do, she looked for different ways of accessing her pupils' skills and knowledge. The teacher recognized that causing my son to repeat or continually revisit his failure ... 3a, 3b, 3a, 3b ... would offer him no opportunity to move on; the teacher also recognized there was more than one way to help children learn to read.

Supporting progression

Finding ways of helping learners engage with common skills and concepts through different tasks and different contexts is vital if learners are to make progress; if they are to make sense of what they are learning. Helping pupils become evermore confident, independent learners and seeing how common skills emerge in different ways through different problems is a key aspect of teaching.

In a recent conversation with a teaching assistant we were considering this very issue. A concern was about pupils neither remembering nor making connections between the work they carried out one day and something they did the next, or from one week to the next. We discussed the feasibility of pupils spending less time routinely practising a skill and more time making a brief record of what they had done and understood, developmentally, in order to make connections between something they do one week and the next. Such a record might take the form of a spider diagram and below is an example.

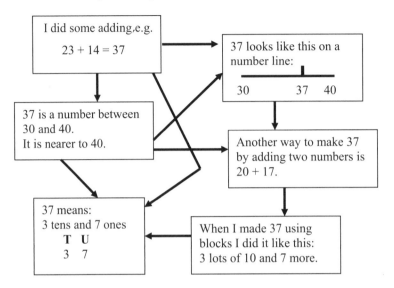

This diagram is intended to be consistent with the quote at the beginning of the chapter, showing a network and possible pathways. Each box on the diagram could be dated and of course put up on the wall as an ongoing piece of display work. The important issue is that of the pupil making a record that helps them not only create a reminder of what they have done and engage in interconnectedness, it also becomes a visual image of real achievement.

Planning for progression and differentiated learning

Whenever a problem opens up a pathway of progression, this enables the potential for differentiated learning opportunities. This is because the teacher can see how a task might be developed and used to help pupils make connections and engage with complexity. This, in turn, is fundamentally what differentiated learning is all about. The following quote from HMI *Mathematics from 5 to 16* (1985: 26) supports this view:

Differentiation of content, if well planned, facilitates progression for all pupils.

Differentiated learning, however, happens in all classrooms not just because of what the teacher does, but also in spite of or sometimes irrespective of what the teacher does. Different pupils will understand something differently, whether this is a different 'take', at a different speed or to a different depth; this is undeniable. Therefore, it is important to offer pupils tasks that naturally cater for such differences to emerge.

From straws to a quadratic via counting and multiplication

The first idea I offer to illustrate this connection between planning for progression and differentiated learning opportunities is based upon the use of coloured straws; placing them in parallel either/or horizontally and vertically. The initial rule I choose to use is that the straws must be arranged to form crossing or intersection points unless all of the straws are placed parallel to each other, in which case there will be zero crossings.

In the diagram below there are seven horizontal straws and three vertical straws, thus forming 21 crossing points. An initial problem could be to find all the other diagrams for ten straws.

Viewed from left to right, there are three lots of seven crossing points, which is 7 × 3 crossing points.

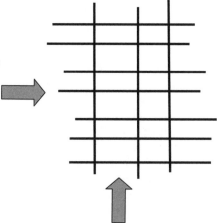

Viewed from bottom to top, there are seven lots of three crossing points, which is 3 × 7 crossing points.

As in many cases with regard to planning and subsequent interactions in the classroom, the teacher must decide how structured they need to make a task. This is particularly so if the task has degrees of openness and, therefore, requires pupils to make decisions about how they might proceed.

At a simple level, once a specific example has been offered, the challenge for some pupils is to count all the crossings: one, two, three … At another level pupils may see this as a multiplication task. Determining what different pupils understand and how they make sense of any problem they are asked to solve is complex and, therefore, it is important to provide pupils with opportunities to demonstrate or to explain what they have understood.

By asking pupils to record all the possible arrangements this will produce partitions of 10; a progression at this juncture can be to turn each partition into coordinate pairs. Graphing these will produce $H + V = 10$ (or $x + y = 10$) as illustrated below.

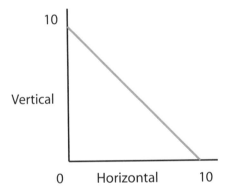

The table below is a collection of the results, in a systematic order. I have produced it only to demonstrate the variety of extension ideas that can accrue from the 'straws' task. While I have produced it here for the purpose of clarity, I would be highly circumspect about giving this as a blank table for pupils to fill in. This is because by providing a table, I would be doing much of the organizational part of the task for the pupils, thus negating the need for pupils to organize the information independently. This, in turn, can reduce pupils' opportunities to be problem solvers as a vitally important aspect of learning mathematics and sense making per se. Deciding how best to organize information is an important aspect of decision making;

the more explicit I am about how pupils might proceed with a task, the less pupils need to think for themselves. There is, of course, a delicate balance to consider, but then teaching is largely about balance, about choosing when to intervene and when to stand back, when to be didactic and when to be ambiguous.

Here is the table:

Horizontal Straws (H)	Vertical Straws (V)	Number of Intersections (I)	(H, V)	(H, I)
0	10	0	(0, 10)	(0, 0)
1	9	9	(1, 9)	(1, 9)
2	8	16	(2, 8)	(2, 16)
3	7	21	(3, 7)	(3, 21)
4	6	24	(4, 6)	(4, 24)
5	5	25	(5, 5)	(5, 25)
6	4	24	(6, 4)	(6, 24)
7	3	21	(7, 3)	(7, 21)
8	2	16	(8, 2)	(8, 16)
9	1	9	(9, 1)	(9, 9)
10	0	0	(10, 0)	10, 0)

By observing differences between adjacent entries in the Intersection column, the following emerge: +9, +7, +5 . . . −7 and −9. The intersections, therefore, form a quadratic sequence and by plotting these as coordinates we can generate the graph:

$$I = 10H - H^2 \text{ (or } y = 10x - x^2).$$

This task has an obvious development about varying the number of straws and this will provide pupils with plenty of practise with the different skills suggested above. Further questions about how to maximize the number of intersections for a given number of straws are aimed at causing pupils to form two generalities, one for an even and one for an odd amount of straws.

There are still further developments, such as if we count the number of spaces enclosed by four lines in the (3, 7) straws diagram above; there are 12 such spaces.

The generality for the number of closed spaces (S_4) is another quadratic generated by the equation $C = (H - 1)(V - 1)$ and because for ten straws $V = 10 - H$, we can write the equation in terms of C and H as $S_4 = (H - 1)(9 - H)$.

By returning to the (3, 7) diagram we can also observe there are some spaces that are not completely bound with four lines, that is spaces with three lines (S_3) and spaces with just two lines (S_2). There are 16 spaces with three lines and these are determined, algebraically, by $S_3 = 2(H - 1) + 2(V - 1)$, or $2H + 2V - 4$, which is, of course, a linear function. For two line spaces, there will always be four of these (unless all ten straws placed horizontally or vertically); here is a constant function $S_2 = 4$.

From a simple situation of placing and counting straws we can generate different quadratic and linear functions and a constant function. In terms of tracking progression, the following content list emerges:

- counting
- number bonds to 10
- multiplying
- plotting coordinate pairs
- drawing linear and quadratic graphs
- determining constant, linear and quadratic functions.

In terms of process skills, there are opportunities for pupils to work systematically and order information. Should they make independent decisions to draw up a table similar to the one above and choose to graph any of the information, this would demonstrate independence and an ability to engage with valuable thinking skills.

From clock faces to decimal time

The next activity is an exploration of 'time' and, as with many of the ideas in this book, I consider the complexities therein. Time is a concept that uses a range of different number bases as well as a deal of different vocabulary. I have a personal concern that 'time' is taught at too early an age and in order to do this there are dangers of oversimplification and, therefore, the potential for misconceptions to grow.

In terms of the different bases used, we have seconds to minutes in base 60, minutes to hours also in base 60, hours to days in base 24 or even base 12 twice over. From days to weeks we are obviously in base 7. After this it becomes 'messy' because there are no fixed bases to convert weeks to months or days to years, well not unless we contemplate an approximation to base 365 and a quarter!

Regarding the vocabulary of time, we talk about 'o'clock', 'five past', 'ten past', 'quarter past', 'twenty past', 'twenty-five past', 'half past', 'twenty-five to', 'twenty to', 'quarter to', 'ten to' and 'five to'. Some of these phrases refer to a certain number of minutes after the hour and some refer to minutes approaching the next hour. Some phrases, however, refer to fractional amounts, 1/4, 1/2 and 3/4. The complexity here is that, for example, five past is when the 'big' hand is pointing towards the 1. Mathematically speaking, the 1 is 1/12 of 60 (or 5). However, at a quarter past, the big hand is pointing to the 3. Thus, there is a mixed vocabulary of numbers and of fractional amounts. For a young child to understand that 1 refers to five past requires knowledge that the 1, as an hour measure, means 5 as a minute measure. Thus, we have two different bases operating simultaneously depending upon which hand is pointing to which number ... confused? Then what about young children's potential confusions?

I was recently asked to develop some ideas for working on 'time' with a KS1 class. The best idea I was able to come up with was to provide the children with the template below copied onto an A4-size piece of card. I call this the 'exploded clock'.

What I sought to achieve with this exploded clock idea was to:

- pose the children a problem that they could play around with
- provide a task they could work on together
- see each other's solutions
- give them a first-hand experience of making a clock face.

I copied the following exploded clock onto three different colours of card with the idea that children could share their cutting out in a group of three so everyone would be able to make a multi-coloured clock face. Once they had cut out and swapped pieces, they were posed the problem of making a clock face. By letting them use blue-tac instead of glue to stick their numbers around their empty clock face, they could make several attempts to place the numbers, intentionally as equally spaced as they could manage. Clearly the process of equally spacing the numbers in a circle is an important one, yet only becomes needful when the children are given such a problem to solve; both myself and the class teacher were intrigued in the way some chose not to equally space the numbers. This alone made it clear

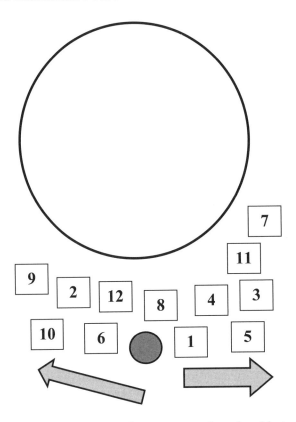

that some of them were nowhere near ready to be able to take on board the concept of time. Putting the hands on was a further task and they were challenged to make different 'o'clock' times and we talked about what they might be doing at different o'clock times.

Because each number on a 12-hour analogue clock stands for three different values, according to whether the big or the little hand is pointing towards a number and whether it is before or after noon, there are even more complexities that children are required to engage with. Just making a clock face in the first instance, therefore, is a worthy challenge. At what point different children are intellectually capable of understanding that every number on a clock face takes on three different meanings is not an easy issue to deal with.

Further complexities emerge, however, because the two hands move at different speeds; the larger one at 12 times a greater speed than the smaller one. A seemingly simple concept such as half past the hour therefore holds its own challenge; while the big hand has moved from the 12 to the 6, the small hand has only moved the equivalent of '2½ minutes'. However, although both hands move together (at different speeds), when the big hand has moved 30 minutes, the big hand has only moved halfway between two of the numbers. With all this complexity around I would suggest that learning to tell the time is something that needs to be worked on very slowly and very carefully and most certainly cannot be rushed into at too early an age.

As with all problems that are worth posing which provide learners with opportunities to work mathematically at different speeds and to different depths, where the minute and hour hands point to at different times of the day is no exception. I complete the ideas for this chapter by posing one further 'time' problem, which would be suitable for KS3 and above. This is an exploration about the times, over a 12-hour period, when the hands are 180° apart. At the outset, the answers may appear obvious, for example 1:35, 2:40, 3:45 and so on. However, these answers are incorrect, because at 1:35 the hands are not 180° apart. Because the hour hand has moved a fractional amount beyond halfway between the 1 and the 2 the angle (measured clockwise) is therefore slightly less than 180°. This problem is intended to cause students to work with degrees of accuracy, preferably to the nearest second and this creates its own challenge. Similar problems might be to work out when the hour and the minute hands are on top of one another, or when they are at 90° to one another.

In conclusion, progression in learning mathematics is about networks and pathways rather than something that can be described in a linear, step-by-step, framework. Helping learners construct their networks and the pathways that connect their networks together is a considerable challenge. This challenge can be met by offering pupils problem-solving tasks to enable them to work on unstructured problems, where they are encouraged to think logically, to draw upon existing knowledge, to create order, look for pattern and seek generality. Developing a culture where pupils expect to use their initiative to develop problems themselves or to be provided with extension ideas by their teacher is a key component of such a culture. By utilizing more open, problem-solving approaches in the mathematics class-room, this challenge becomes not only more achievable but also a more interesting way of learning and teaching mathematics.

The more challenges we offer pupils and the more they learn to embrace such challenges, in positive ways, the more interesting and effective places for the learning of mathematics our classrooms can become. The strategies and resources we use to structure pupils' learning experiences so they not only achieve as mathematicians, but also learn how to recognize progression in their learning, is a central theme of this book.

In the final chapter I focus on resources for teaching mathematics.

Resources to support the teaching and learning of mathematics

In this final chapter, I have collected together an index of resources. I have not included any IT resources and this is for two reasons. The first is that there is an awful lot of rubbish out there and were I to compile a shortlist of software I have used, I would not wish to suggest that what does not appear is, by implication, unworthy. Second, and you can call me old-fashioned, but I think children spend enough time in front of flashing screens, in virtual worlds, at PlayStations and watching interactive whiteboards; so much potential and so much passivity. I am far more interested in advocating the use of resources that have stood the test of time, Cuisenaire, linking cubes, geoboards, different grid papers and so on; resources that pupils can play with, work with and draw on. The resources I describe are inexpensive and can be used in a range of settings from Foundation stage to post-16 classrooms. On this basis I offer you a list of resources, in alphabetical order, that I have used. For each resource I list typical tasks and concepts that have the potential to be developed.

ATM mats
These are a set of regular polygons (apart from the oblong) made out of beer-mat type card and can be joined together to make 2D tessellation patterns and 3D solids with a thin film of Copydex glue.

   Suggested texts: *Shapes in Space*; *100+ Ideas for Teaching Mathematics*.

Cuisenaire rods
Brightly coloured rods that are starting to come back into

fashion. Useful for work with Foundation stage children for number recognition, partitioning, making number sentences, using symbols, group theory for undergraduate level.

Suggested text: *Primary Idea Book for Cuisenaire Rods*.

Dice

Lots and lots of simple games and puzzles can be created with dice. Using blank dice you can write your own numbers on the faces. Probability experiments (usual suspects).

Suggested texts: *Mathematical Activities from Poland*; *The Bumper Book of Indoor Games*.

Suggested source: Your local 'pound' shop (five dice, two packs of cards and a set of 6-6 dominoes all for £1).

Dienes base 10 blocks

Many primary schools will have a box of base 10 equipment. Sadly they often inhabit the back of store cupboards, collecting dust. They are a fantastic resource for helping pupils make sense of the place value system and can be used for addition, subtraction, multiplication and division.

Suggested source: Educational equipment catalogues.

Dominoes

Useful for number recognition, counting, sequencing, fractions and playing lots of different games (see Chapter 8).

Suggested texts: *Mathematical Activities from Poland*; *The Bumper Book of Indoor Games*.

Suggested source: Your local 'pound' shop.

Geoboards (square nine-pin)

For use in KS1 to KS5 classrooms, this is an essential piece of kit for developing vast swathes of the geometry (shape, space and measures) attainment target, as well as algebra, surds ... Make a class set and don't forget the elastic bands.

Suggested text: *Using Geoboards*; *100+ Ideas for Teaching Mathematics*.

Suggested source: *www.cleo.net.uk/*

Geoboards (circular)

I have made circular boards with nine and ten pins on the circumference and one pin in the middle. Were I to prioritize some time to make some more I would also create 12-pin boards. Useful for making triangles and cyclic quadrilaterals, and to consider how to code the shapes made. Clear opportunities to emerge for working on circle/angle theorems.

Suggested text: *100+ Ideas for Teaching Mathematics*.

Geostrips

These are different coloured and different length plastic strips that have holes through which to place split-pins to join them together. Lots of shape-making possibilities and classifying their properties.

Suggested text: *Everyone Is Special*.

Linking cubes

As with pegs and pegboards, linking cubes can be used for counting and grouping purposes and for generating sequences. They can also be used for creating probability type experiments and of course to work on concepts of surface area and volume.

Suggested text: *Linking Cubes and the Learning of Mathematics*.

Pegs and pegboards

From KS1 to KS5 classrooms pegs and pegboards can be used for counting, making grouping patterns, making shapes, to create reflective and rotational design patterns, to make coordinate designs, to create numerical sequences, to play the game of 'frogs', the game of 'nim', the game of 'four in a line' and, as described in Chapter 7, we can suggest tasks that would challenge KS5 students.

Pentagon triangles

These are the three isosceles triangles formed from the dissection of a regular pentagon. Useful for putting together to make other shapes (KS1) to creating values in the Fibonacci sequence (KS3).

Playing cards

As with dominoes, playing cards are useful for counting, number bonds, playing lots of games, doing card tricks.

Suggested text: *The Bumper Book of Indoor Games*.

Suggested sources: Your local 'pound' shop and find out what your local Bridge club do with their used packs.

Straws

They can be bundled together into piles of tens and ten piles of tens as a way into place value. I offer a problem using straws in

Chapter 9. They can also be used to make 3D skeleton solids with pipe cleaners to join them together.

Source: Educational equipment catalogues.

Grid papers

The following list of grid papers are the ones I have used either in conjunction with some of the manipulatives mentioned above or for specific tasks. Having speedy access to a range of grid papers is important; having to trail next door, 'nip' to the photocopier or go down the corridor to the stock cupboard will not create a conducive climate for their use. My list contains:

- 1cm square dot
- 1cm isometric dot
- 1.5cm isometric
- multiple nine-dot grids (for use with geoboards)
- multiple 16-dot, 25-dot grids
- tessellation grids (see *The tessellations file*, Tarquin Publications)
- 45° 45° 90° tessellation grid
- 30° 60° 90° tessellation grid (see *Everyone is special*, ATM: 14)
- multiple circular dot grids (9, 10, 12 plus one in the middle)
- 1cm-squared paper
- 2cm-squared paper
- square paper and card cut from A5 (for origami type ideas)
- fractions to decimals grid (see *Everyone is special*, ATM: 7)
- rotating arm grid (see Chapter 4)
- place value grids (see Introductory chapter).

Other essential equipment

As well as the obvious such as scissors, glue, glue pots, glue sticks, card, protractors and pairs of compasses, I suggest the following:

- A4, A5, A6 and A7 paper (for all kind of 2D and 3D shape/solid making and fractions).
- Card cut into the dimensions of $1:\sqrt{3}$ (for making tetrahedrons and octahedrons).
- Collect waste A4 card and paper and cut them into strips, approx 2.5cm wide – great for making fraction walls and other many other uses.
- Retain the strip when making squares cut from A5 paper/card – use four different colours to make the 'Cairo' tiling design.

To complete this chapter, and the book, I raise the question:

'Why use resources?' This is because I believe it is important to rationalize what part resources and manipulatives might play in the learning of mathematics.

Why use resources?

With regard to using resources, I wish to raise two questions about the value any resource has in terms of helping pupils learn mathematics. When we ask pupils to fold a piece of paper and then do some thinking or answer some questions or carry out a further task with the said folded piece of paper, what purpose does such an event serve? How does the action of folding a piece of paper support pupils' understanding? How does folding a piece of paper, perhaps in order to gain an understanding about working with fractions, help anyone answer questions on fractions in an examination?

There is a conflict here between learners gaining an in-depth understanding of a concept or a superficial understanding based upon received methods and routines offered to learners in order to gain correct answers when applied to questions from a textbook, a worksheet or in an examination. An approach to teaching that is predominantly about providing examples, methods and routines, followed by pupils practising these routines over and over, is possibly the approach that causes so many people to dislike mathematics and feel it makes little sense.

If superficial learning is about remembering the steps we need to take in order to answer a specific type of question, then in-depth learning is underpinned by recognizing when to apply certain knowledge to a situation, which may not immediately be an obvious or a familiar one. When pupils are asked to 'prove' something or demonstrate they know why something works then, I suggest, the conditions for deep learning are likely to exist.

For deep learning to take place, pupils need to have first-hand experiences to support their explorations. They need access to resources to do something with, in order to promote discussion about ideas and about mathematical structures. Learners need to be presented with problems that require more than one or two specific steps to reach a solution and to explore links between concepts. Deep learning requires pupils to ask questions, to prove how and why something works. When concepts become evident-to-self, then learning is based upon firm foundations;

once this happens we can become more confident to take further steps and become more independent learners.

Clearly resources are not imbued with mystical powers that guarantee the user will achieve enlightenment; it is all about how a resource is used and what the teacher's intentions are when deciding to use a particular resource . . . or as Anne Watson sang at the 2008 Joined-Up mathematics conference at Keele University:

'taint what you do it's the way you do it.
'taint what you learn it's the way that you learn it.
'taint what you teach it's the way you teach it.

Glossary

Quick glossary of terms

AfL	Assessment for learning.
AST	Advanced skills teacher.
Attainment targets	These define the knowledge, skills and level of understanding that pupils of different abilities and levels of maturity are expected to have by the end of each Key Stage.
BECTA	British Educational Communications and Technology Agency: the UK government's leading Agency for information and communications technology (ICT) in education.
BT	Beginning teacher: a teacher who is working in a school as part of their initial teacher training (ITT).
CACHE	Council for awards in children's care and education.
CAL	Computer aided learning: applies to any learning experience that has been enhanced or supported by the use of computers.
CATs	Cognitive ability tests: an assessment of a range of reasoning skills.
CEDP	Career entry and development profile: used by all new teachers to chart their progression through their teaching career.
CPD	Continuing professional development.
CPO	Child protection officer.
Core subjects	English, maths and science: as part of the National Curriculum, all pupils must study these subjects up to Key Stage 4 (age 16).

CRB disclosure   Criminal records bureau disclosure: it is a legal requirement that all teachers are checked against CRB records to determine their suitability to work with young people.

Curriculum   The range and content of subjects taught within school.

DCSF   Department for Children, Schools and Families. Formerly known as the education and children's services department of the DfES. Government department that regulates all areas of education and the National Curriculum.

Differentiation   Differentiation involves teaching the same curriculum to students of all ranges and abilities using teaching strategies and resources to meet the varied needs of each individual.

DT   Design technology.

Diagnostic testing   A form of assessment that highlights specific areas of strength or weakness.

E2E   Entry to employment: schemes and training opportunities working in partnership with schools and local authorities to provide suitable life skills, education and training to pupils who may have been excluded or gained very few qualifications.

EAL   English as an additional language.

EAZs   Education action zones: based around primary and some secondary schools. Support can include: school-home support workers, extra-curricular activity centres, homework support groups in local libraries and so on.

EBD   Emotional and behavioural difficulties/disorder.

EdPsyc   Educational psychologist.

EMA   Education maintenance allowance: a fortnightly payment of up to £60 for students who are aged 16–19 who stay on in education after they reach the end of their compulsory schooling.

EMAG   The ethnic minority achievement grant: government money for supporting schools and local authorities to meet the educational needs of minority ethnic pupils.

ESOL   English for speakers of other languages.

EWO/ESW   Educational welfare officer/social worker: a

	person responsible for ensuring pupils' regular attendance at school and other related issues.
GCSE	General Certificate of Secondary Education: the national examination that students usually take in several subjects at age 16.
GNVQ	General national vocational qualification: courses in vocational subjects such as art and design, health and social care and so on.
G&T	Gifted and talented.
GTC	General teaching council.
GTTR	Graduate teacher training registry.
HMI	Her Majesty's Inspector of schools employed by Ofsted.
HoD	Head of department (sometimes known as head of subject).
HoY	Head of year (group).
ICT	Information and communications technology.
IEP	Individual education plan: a programme of support for pupils with a statement of special educational needs.
In loco parentis	Means 'in place of a parent'; the legal term defining teachers' responsibility for pupils in their care.
INSET	In-service education and training for school staff.
ITT	Initial teacher training: the period during which a teacher undertakes training to achieve qualified teacher status (QTS).
Key Stages	The National Curriculum is divided into four main stages:

	Key Stage 1	Key Stage 2	Key Stage 3	Key Stage 4
Age	5–7	7–11	11–14	14–16
Year groups	1–2	3–6	7–9	10–11

LA/LEA	Local authority/local education authority: a division of the local government with specific responsibility for education.
LSA and LST	Learning support assistant and learning support teacher: support staff for pupils with special educational needs, often works with individual children in class or within designated learning support units.
LSU	Learning support unit: a department within a

school set up to help students with learning and/or behavioural difficulties.

MFL — Modern foreign languages.

NT — National tests (formerly standard assessment tests SATs): tests used to show your child's progress compared with other children born in the same month. Tests taken at Key Stages 1, 2 and 3 cover the three core subjects; English, maths and science. GCSEs are taken at the end of KS4.

Key Stage	Age National Test taken	Published
1	7	No
2	11	Yes
3	14	No
4	16	Yes

NLS — National Literacy Strategy.

NNS — National Numeracy Strategy.

NQT — Newly qualified teacher: a person in his or her first year of teaching who has successfully completed their teacher training.

NRA — National record of achievement: a personalized folder detailing a student's achievement and attainment throughout their (secondary) school career.

Objectives — Goals, results or improvements that the decision maker wants to attain.

Ofsted — Office for Standards in Education: the organization who is responsible for school inspections and assess the quality and standards of education.

PANDA — Performance and assessment: a report generated by Ofsted to allow schools to assess their performance and make comparisons with other schools nationally.

PAT — Pupil achievement tracker: a piece of diagnostic and analytical software produced by the DCSF/DfES to enable students' performance and attainment to be tracked.

Pedagogy — Refers to the art or science of teaching, but also describes the strategies, techniques and approaches that teachers can use to facilitate learning.

Performance tables	The collected statistics for schools and local authorities such as results of national examinations and absence data and so on, published by the DCSF.
PPA	Planning, preparation and assessment: at least 10 per cent of every teacher's timetable should be free for PPA time.
Programmes of study	The content of teaching programmes laid down in the National Curriculum for each subject.
PSE or PHSE	Personal and social education or personal, social and health education.
PSP	Personal support plan: personalized targets to support pupils often on the verge of exclusion
PTA	Parent/teacher association.
QCA	Qualifications and Curriculum Authority, the body that develops the curriculum and its assessment.
QTS	Qualified teacher status: qualification gained after successfully completing a period of teacher training needed to work in any state-maintained school.
SEN	Special educational needs: a term used to describe a range of conditions within three main categories: learning difficulties, behaviour difficulties or physical and medical difficulties.
SENCO	Special educational needs coordinator: the teacher with responsibility for SEN pupils within a school.
SMART targets	Specific, measurable, achievable, realistic and time-related: helping to monitor how targets and goals viewed and completed.
SLT	Senior leadership team.
SMT	Senior management team: the leading members of a school or education provider.
TDA	Teacher Development Agency, also know as Training and Development Agency for Schools (formerly the TTA – teacher training agency).
TLR	Teaching and learning responsibilities: responsibilities that impact positively on educational progress beyond the teacher's assigned role.
VAK	Visual, auditory and kinesthetic learning styles model refers to the preferred learning style of an individual and focuses on 'active' teaching and learning strategies.

Education and government

Department for Schools, Children and Families (DCSF)
📧 Sanctuary Buildings, Great Smith Street, London SW1P 3BT
☎ 0870 000 2288 💻 www.dcsf.gov.uk

Department for Education in Northern Ireland
📧 Rathgael House, Balloo Road, Bangor BT19 7PR
☎ 028 9127 9279 💻 www.deni.gov.uk

HM Inspectorate of Education (HMIE)
📧 Denholm House, Almondvale Business Park, Almondvale Way, Livingston EH54 6GA
☎ 01506 600 200 💻 www.hmie.gov.uk

Office for Standards in Education, Children's Services and Skills (OfSTED)
📧 Royal Exchange Buildings, St Ann's Square, Manchester M2 7LA
☎ 08456 404045 💻 www.ofsted.gov.uk

Scottish Executive Education Department
📧 School Education, The Scottish Government, Victoria Quay, Edinburgh EH6 6QQ
☎ 0131 556 8400 💻 www.scotland.gov.uk/Topics/Education

Welsh Assembly Government Education and Skills
📧 Minister for Children, Education, Lifelong Learning & Skills, Welsh Assembly Government, Cardiff Bay, Cardiff CF99 1NA
☎ 0845 010 3300 💻 New.wales.gov.uk/topics/educationand skills

What is a LA?
In England and Wales, local authorities (LAs) are responsible for managing all state schools within their area. Responsibilities include funding, allocation of places and teacher employment. You can locate your local authority via DSCF: www.schools-web.gov.uk/locate/management/lea/fylea

What are GTCs?
The General Teaching Councils are independent professional bodies with statutory power to advise the government on teaching. All qualified teachers in the UK working in state schools are required to register with a GTC.

GTC for England

✉ Whittington House, 19-30 Alfred Place, London WC1E 7EA

☎ 0870 001 0308　　💻 www.gtce.org.uk

GTC for Northern Ireland

✉ 4th Floor Albany House, 73–75 Great Victoria Street, Belfast BT2 7AF

☎ 028 9033 3390　　💻 www.gtcni.org.uk

GTC for Scotland

✉ Clerwood House, 96 Clermiston Road, Edinburgh EH12 6UT

☎ 0131 314 6000　　💻 www.gtcs.org.uk

GTC for Wales

✉ 4th Floor, Southgate House, Wood Street, Cardiff CF10 1EW

☎ 029 20550350　　💻 www.gtcw.org.uk

Teacher training

Administration

Graduate Teacher Training Registry (GTTR)

Responsible for processing applications for PGCE and PGDE courses in England and Wales, and Scotland.

✉ Rosehill, New Barn Lane, Cheltenham, Gloucestershire GL52 3LZ

☎ 0871 468 0469　　💻 www.gttr.ac.uk

Training and Development Agency for Schools (TDA)

Government agency responsible for training and development of teaching workforce.

✉ 151 Buckingham Palace Road, London SW1W 9SZ

☎ 0845 6000 991　　💻 www.tda.gov.uk

Training routes

Who needs QTS?

Anyone wishing to teach in a state school in England and Wales needs to achieve **Qualified teacher status (QTS)**. All the training routes shown lead to QTS or equivalent.

There is no QTS in Scotland, however, new teaching graduates are required to complete an induction year and register with the GTCS.

Bachelor of education (BEd)

An honours degree course in education. Courses enable students to study for their degree and complete initial teacher training at the same time. A popular choice in teaching primary school children: ⊘ 3–4 years.

Graduate teacher programme (GTP)

Trainees are employed by a school as unqualified teachers. On-the-job training is tailored to individual needs: ⊘ 1 year.

Postgraduate certificate in education (PGCE)

Trainees spend at least a third of their time studying at a higher education institution and two thirds on three or more teaching placements in local schools. Teaching placements usually last from two to seven weeks: ⊘ 1 year.

Postgraduate diploma of education (PGDE)

Similar to a PGCE, but followed by students in Scotland: ⊘ 1 year.

Registered teacher programme (RTP)

Training route for non-graduates, providing a blend of work-based teacher training and academic study, enabling trainees to complete their degree and qualify as a teacher at the same time: ⊘ 2 years.

School-centred initial teacher training (SCITT)

Trainees spend more time training in the classroom and are taught by experienced, practising teachers. Training is delivered by groups of neighbouring schools and colleges. May also lead to PGCE: ⊘ 1 year.

Teach First

Programme aimed to encourage top graduates to consider teaching as a career. Trainees work in challenging secondary schools receiving teacher and leadership training, as well as work experience with leading employers: ⊘ 2 years.

Pay and conditions

How does a new teacher's salary grow?

Newly qualified teachers are placed on the **main pay scale** (salary scale for classroom teachers in Scotland) at a point dependent on relevant career experience. Salary increases by one increment each year subject to satisfactory performance.

England & Wales: main pay scale (From 1 September 2008)

Spine Point	Inner London	Outer London	Other
M1	£25,000	£24,000	£20,627
M2	£26,581	£25,487	£22,259
M3	£28,261	£27,065	£24,048
M4	£30,047	£28,741	£25,898
M5	£32,358	£31,178	£27,939
M6	£34,768	£33,554	£30,148

What is the STRB?

The **school teachers' review body (STRB)** reports to the Secretary of State for Education making recommendations on teachers' pay and conditions in England and Wales.

What about teachers in Northern Ireland?

Teachers' pay scales in Northern Ireland are generally the same as those in England and Wales.

Scotland: Salary scale for classroom teachers (From 1 April 2008)

Scale Point	Salary
0	£20,427
1	£24,501
2	£25,956
3	£27,432
4	£29,025
5	£30,864
6	£32,583

What happens when you reach the top of the scale?

In England and Wales, teachers who reach the top of the main pay scale can apply to cross the 'threshold' and move to the upper pay scale. In Scotland, teachers can apply to become chartered teachers when they reach the top of the salary scale.

Unions

Should I join a union?

Union membership is strongly recommended. Teaching is a demanding profession with many potential legal minefields. Teaching unions provide legal and professional advice, guidance and support.

What are the benefits of TUC affiliation?

Most unions are affiliated to the trades union congress (TUC) and members benefit from being part of a larger organization. Independent unions typically cater for more specialized professions and are not bound by inter-union agreements or political affiliations.

Association of Teachers & Lecturers (ATL)

Represents teachers and lecturers in England, Wales and Northern Ireland. TUC affiliated.

- 7 Northumberland Street, London WC2N 5RD
- ☎ 020 7930 6441   💻 www.atl.org.uk
- 👥 120,000

Educational Institute of Scotland (EIS)

Largest organization of teachers and lecturers in Scotland. TUC affiliated.

- 46 Moray Place, Edinburgh EH3 6BH
- ☎ 0131 225 6244   💻 www.eis.org.uk
- 👥 59,000

National Association of Headteachers (NAHT)

Main association representing the interests of headteachers. Independent.

- 1 Heath Square, Boltro Road, Haywards Heath, West Sussex RH16 1BL
- ☎ 01444 472472   💻 www.naht.org.uk
- 👥 30,000

National Association of School Masters/Union of Women Teachers (NASUWT)

Only TUC affiliated teachers' union representing teachers and headteachers in all parts of the UK.

- Hillscourt Education Centre, Rose Hill, Rednal, Birmingham B45 8RS
- ☎ 0121 453 6150   💻 www.nasuwt.org.uk
- 👥 250,000

National Union of Teachers (NUT)
Largest teaching union representing teachers and headteachers. TUC affiliated.
☎ Hamilton House, Mabledon Place, London WC1H 9BD
☎ 020 7388 6191   💻 www.teachers.org.uk
👥 270,000

University and College Union (UCU)
Largest trade union and professional association for academics, lecturers, trainers, researchers and academic-related staff. TUC affiliated.
☎ 27 Britannia Street, London WC1X 9JP
☎ 020 7837 3636   💻 www.ucu.org.uk
👥 120,000

Voice Formerly the Professional Association of Teachers (PAT)
Independent trade union representing teachers, headteachers, lecturers, teaching assistants, technicians, administrators and support staff, in the public and private sectors.
☎ 2 St James' Court, Friar Gate, Derby DE1 1BT
☎ 01332 372 337   💻 www.voicetheunion.org.uk
👥 35,000

Curriculum qualifications

England, Wales & Northern Ireland

SAT	Statutory Assessment Tasks
GCSE	General Certificate of Secondary Education
BTEC	Business & Technician Education Council
NVQ	National Vocational Qualification
A Level	Advanced Level
A/S	Advanced Subsidiary Level

Scotland

Standard Grade	
Higher	
Advanced Higher	
SVQ	Scottish Vocational Qualification

NQF and SCQF

What is the NQF?

The **National Qualifications Framework (NQF)** and **Scottish Credit and Qualifications Framework (SCQF)** group together qualifications that place similar demands on learners.

NQF and SCQF equivalent qualifications

NQF Level	Qualifications	Vocational Qualifications
1	GCSE (grades D–G)	BTEC Introductory Diploma
		NVQ
2	GCSEs (grades A*–C)	BTEC First Diploma
		NVQ
3	A level	BTEC Diploma
	International Baccalaureate	BTEC National

SCQF Level	Qualification	Vocational Qualification
3	Foundation Standard Grade	
4	General Standard Grade	SVQ1
5	Credit Standard Grade	SVQ2
6	Higher	SVQ3
7	Advanced Higher	

Subject associations

Association for Science Education
College Lane, Hatfield, Hertfordshire AL10 9AA
01707 283000   www.ase.org.uk

Association for Teachers of Mathematics
Unit 7 Prime Industrial Park, Shaftesbury Street, Derby DE23 8YB
01332 346599   www.atm.org.uk

Centre for Information on Language Teaching and Research
3rd Floor, 111 Westminster Bridge Road, London SE1 7HR
020 7379 5101   www.cilt.org.uk

Economics and Business Studies Association (EBEA)
The Forum, 277 London Road, Burgess Hill RH15 9QU
01444 240150   www.ebea.org.uk

Geographical Association
160 Solly Street, Sheffield S1 4BF
0114 296 0088   www.geography.org.uk

Historical Association
59a Kennington Park Road, London SE11 4JH
020 7735 3901   www.history.org.uk

National Association for Advisors and Inspectors in Design and Technology

📠 68 Brookfield Crescent, Hampsthwaite, Harrogate, North Yorkshire HG3 2EE

☎ www.naaidt.org.uk

National Association for the Teaching of English (NATE)

📠 50 Broadfield Road, Sheffield, South Yorkshire S8 OXJ

☎ 0114 255 5419   💻 www.nate.org.uk

RE Today

📠 1020 Bristol Road, Selly Oak, Birmingham B29 6LB

☎ 0121 472 4242   💻 www.retoday.org.uk

Exam boards

Assessment & Qualifications Alliance (AQA)

📠 Guildford Office Stag Hill House, Guildford, Surrey GU2 7XJ
Harrogate Office 31-33 Springfield Avenue, Harrogate, North Yorkshire HG1 2HW
Manchester Office Devas Street, Manchester M15 6EX

☎ Guildford 01483 506 506
Harrogate 01423 840 015
Manchester 0161 953 1180 💻 www.aqa.org.uk

Northern Ireland Council for the Curriculum, Examination and Assessment (CCEA)

📠 29 Clarendon Road, Clarendon Dock, Belfast BT1 3BG

☎ 02890 261200   💻 www.ccea.org.uk

City & Guilds

📠 1 Giltspur Street, London EC1A 9DD

☎ 020 7294 2800   💻 www.cityandguilds.com

Edexcel

📠 Edexcel Customer Service, One90 High Holborn, London WC1V 7BH.

☎ 0844 576 0025   💻 www.edexcel.org.uk

London Chamber of Commerce and Industry Examinations Board (LCCIEB)

☎ 08707 202909   💻 www.lccieb.com

Oxford, Cambridge and RSA Examinations (OCR)

📠 1 Hills Road, Cambridge CB1 2EU

☎ 01223 553 998   💻 www.ocr.org.uk

Scottish Qualifications Authority (SQA)
▭ The Optima Building, 58 Robertson Street, Glasgow G2 8DQ
☎ 0845 279 1000   ▭ www.sqa.org.uk

Welsh Joint Education Committee (WJEC)
▭ 245 Western Avenue, Cardiff CF5 2YX
☎ 029 2026 5000   ▭ www.wjec.co.uk

Media

General media

BBC News	www.bbc.co.uk/learning/subjects/schools
Daily Telegraph	www.telegraph.co.uk/education
Guardian	education.guardian.co.uk
Independent	www.independent.co.uk/news/education
Times	www.timesonline.co.uk/tol/life_and_style/education
TES	www.tes.co.uk

Teachers TV

Freesat	650
Freeview	88
Sky	880
Tiscali TV	845
Virgin TV	240

Lesson planning

What is a learning style?

A learning style is the method of educating which best suits an individual. Teachers are encouraged to assess and adapt to the learning styles of their pupils. Common learning style definitions are shown below.

Auditory: learning occurs through hearing the spoken word.
Kinesthetic: learning occurs through doing and interacting.
Visual: learning occurs through looking at images, demonstrations and body language

Assessment

Formative
Teachers use their assessments (observation, homework, discussion etc) to adapt teaching and learning to meet student needs. Characterized as assessment for learning.

Summative
Students sit a test to assess their progress over a given period. Characterized as assessment of learning.

Inclusion – SEN and other barriers to learning

What do we mean by SEN pupils?
The DCSF defines students with **special educational needs (SEN)** as having 'learning difficulties or disabilities which make it harder for them to learn or access education than most other children of the same age'. School **special educational needs coordinators (SENCO)** are responsible for coordinating SEN provision within a school.

Attention deficit (hyperactivity) disorder (ADHD)
Students have difficulty focusing on a specific task. Easily distracted, they have a very short attention span and have trouble commencing work. Those with hyperactivity may act impulsively and erratically.

Autistic spectrum disorder (ASD)
Students share three main areas of difficulty: i) social communication; ii) social interaction; and iii) social imagination. The condition affects students in different ways, hence use of the word 'spectrum'.

Asperger's syndrome
Form of autism associated with more intellectually-able individuals.

Dyscalculia
Students have difficulty acquiring mathematical skills. They may have difficulty understanding simple number concepts and lack an intuitive grasp of numbers.

Dyslexia

Students have a marked and persistent difficulty in learning to read, write and spell. They may have poor reading comprehension, handwriting and punctuation skills.

Dyspraxia

Students are affected by an impairment or immaturity of the organization of movement and often appear clumsy. They may have poor balance and coordination. Their articulation may also be immature and their language late to develop.

English as an additional language (EAL)/English as a secondary language (ESL)

Students whose main language at home (mother tongue) is a language other than English.

Emotional/behavioural disorder (EBD)

Students' behaviour provides a barrier to their learning despite implementation of effective school behaviour policy.

Hearing impairment (HI)

Students with a hearing impairment range from those with mild hearing loss to those who are profoundly deaf.

Individual education plan (IEP)

Document setting out additional support and strategies provided to meet the needs of a student with learning difficulties.

Moderate learning difficulty (MLD)

In comparison with their peers, students have much greater difficulty acquiring basic literacy and numeracy skills and in understanding concepts. Other difficulties include low self-esteem, low levels of concentration and underdeveloped social skills.

Multi-sensory impairment (MSI)

Students have a combination of visual and hearing difficulties. They may also have additional disabilities.

Physical disability (PD)

Students with a visual, mobility or orthopaedic impairment that impacts on their ability to access the curriculum.

Profound and multiple learning difficulty (PMLD)
In addition to very severe learning difficulties, students have other significant difficulties, such as physical disabilities, sensory impairment or a severe medical condition.

Severe learning difficulty (SLD)
Students have significant intellectual or cognitive impairments. This has a major effect on their ability to participate in the school curriculum without support.

Specific learning difficulty (SpLD)
Umbrella term used to cover a range of difficulties including dyslexia, dyscalculia and dyspraxia.

National SEN Associations

British Dyslexia Association
✉ Unit 8, Bracknell Beeches, Old Bracknell Lane, Bracknell RG12 7BW
☎ 0845 251 9002   www.bdadyslexia.org.uk

National Attention Deficit Disorder Information and Support Service
✉ P.O. Box 340 Edgware, Middlesex HA8 9HL
☎ 020 8952 2800   💻 www.addiss.co.uk

National Association for Language Development in the Curriculum
✉ Serif House, 10 Dudley Street, Luton LU2 0NT
☎ 01582 724724   💻 www.naldic.org.uk

National Autistic Society
✉ 393 City Road, London EC1V 1NG
☎ 020 7833 2299   💻 www.autism.org.uk

National Association for Special Educational Needs
✉ Nasen House, Amber Business Village, Amber Close, Amington, Tamworth, Staffordshire B77 4RP
☎ 01827 311500   💻 www.nasen.org.uk

Dyspraxia Foundation
✉ West Alley, Hitchin, Hertfordshire SG5 1EG
☎ 01462 454 986   💻 www.dyspraxiafoundation.org.uk

Royal National Institute for the Deaf
✉ 19-23 Featherstone Street, London EC1Y 8SL
☎ 0808 808 0123   💻 www.rnid.org.uk

Lesson plans

What should be included?

Many schools and universities have their own recommended lesson-plan format. The suggested structure below provides a possible structure and key areas of content.

Teacher		Date		Subject	
Class		No. Pupils		Ability/Level	
		No. SEN Pupils		**LSA Support**	Y/N

Context	An introduction to… /Builds on material covered in a previous lesson… A cooperative/challenging class… strategies employed include …		
Aim	Why do we … What is the link between…		
Objectives	Understand key features of… Learn how to…		
Outcomes	Write down five facts about… Identify the key features of …	**Keywords**	
Structure		Teaching Activity	Pupil Activities
	Starter		Work in pairs
			Recall previous lesson
	Main Body		Complete exercise
			Work in pairs
	Plenary		Write down
			Discuss

Differentiation	Extension questions Peer support		
Assessment	Teacher led Q&A – targeted and open questions Marking books		
Resources	Text books, PowerPoint		
LSA Support	Focus on pupil x Circulate among all pupils		
SEN Pupils	Name	Condition	**Strategy**
		Dyslexia	Keywords on board LSA help writing h/w

Other useful websites

Site name: A to Z of School Leadership and Management
Description: Advice on legislation concerning schools, and guidance on a range of school-management issues.
URL: www.teachernet.gov.uk/atoz

Site name: Addresses of LAs in England with websites
Description: A comprehensive list of LA contacts, news, information and communications from the DCSF.
URL: www.dfes.gov.uk/localauthorities

Site name: Advanced Skills Teachers
Description: Information from Teachernet for teachers who wish to apply.
URL: www.teachernet.gov.uk/professionaldevelopment/opportunities/ast

Site name: BBC Key Stage 2 Revisewise bitesize revision
Description: Revision work for Key Stage 2 students in English, mathematics and science from the BBC Education website.
URL: www.bbc.co.uk/schools/revisewise

Site name: BECTA – British Educational Communities and Technology Agency
Description: The UK government's leading agency for information and communications technology (ICT) in education.
URL: www.becta.org.uk

Site name: Behaviour and Attendance
Description: Information about the government's programme to improve pupil   behaviour and attendance.
URL: www.dfes.gov.uk/behaviourandattendance/index.cfm

Site name: Birmingham Grid for Learning
Description: The public portal contains resources and links for learners, teachers, parents and administrators.
URL: www.bgfl.org/bgfl/

Site name: Building Bridges
Description: Information on the Independent/State School Partnerships Grant Scheme, set up to encourage collaborative working between independent and maintained schools.
URL: www.dfes.gov.uk/buildingbridges

Site name: CEGNET
Description: Careers education website from the Connexions Service National Unit for schools and colleges and their partners.
URL: www.cegnet.co.uk

Site name: Children and Young People's Unit
Description: The website of the government unit for the better coordination of policies and services for children.
URL: www.allchildrenni.gov.uk/

Site name: Choice
Description: First online course prospectus for 14- to 19-year-olds in London. Includes a free searchable directory of over 25,000 courses with clear details of all the learning opportunities open to young people.
URL: www.yourlondon.gov.uk/choice

Site name: Citizenship
Description: The DCSF citizenship website. Includes schemes of work and teaching resources, plus articles and information from assessment to whole-school issues.
URL: www.dfes.gov.uk/citizenship

Site name: Code of Practice on LA-School Relations
Description: Link to a downloadable version of the code, providing statutory guidance on how to raise standards.
URL: www.dfes.gov.uk/lea

Site name: Connecting Voices (COVO)
Description: A Southwark-based charity delivering services that address conflict, disaffection and underachievement in education and the workplace.
URL: www.covo.org.uk

Site name: Connexions
Description: Guidance and support for 13- to 19-year-olds in all areas of life.
URL: www.connexions.gov.uk

Site name: Curriculum Online
Description: A comprehensive catalogue of digital learning resources for the National Curriculum for England.
URL: www.curriculumonline.gov.uk

Site name: Don't Suffer in Silence

Description: Website showing pupils, their families and teachers how to tackle bullying problems.

URL: www.dfes.gov.uk/bullying

Site name: Education Protects

Description: A project funded by the DCSF aiming to help raise the educational achievements of children and young people in care.

URL: www.dfes.gov.uk/educationprotects

Site name: DCSF – Languages Strategy

Description: The Languages for Life website outlining the government's languages plans to transform language use and acquisition.

URL: www.dfes.gov.uk/ languagesstrategy/

Site name: Directgov

Description: Main portal for access to UK government services, including the latest, up-to-date public-service information.

URL: www.direct.gov.uk

Site name: Every Child Matters: Change for Children

Description: Useful materials and case studies to help understand and deliver the *Every Child Matters* agenda.

URL: www.everychildmatters.gov.uk

Site name: Fast Track

Description: Accelerated leadership development programme for new teachers.

URL: www.dfee.gov.uk/fasttrack

Site name: Global Gateway

Description: Information for the development of an international dimension in education. Including ideas for lesson plans, free downloadable resources, an area for young people and information on gap years.

URL: www.globalgateway.org

Site name: Go-Givers

Description: Site showing primary children what it means to be part of a caring society. Including case studies for assemblies, discussion activities and a range of resources ideal for teaching citizenship.

URL: www.gogivers.org

Site name: Homework: The Standards Site
Description: Support for the development of independent learning skills
                andattitudes for successful lifelong learning.
URL: www.standards.dfes.gov.uk/homework

Site name: Key Stage 3: The Standards Site
Description: Information on the KS3 curriculum standards.
URL: www.standards.dfee.gov.uk/keystage3

Site name: Learning and Skills Council
Description: Information and guidance on further education, work-based
                training, entry to employment and modern apprenticeships.
URL: www.lsc.gov.uk

Site name: Learning and Skills Development Agency
Description: National resource for the development of policy and
                practice in post-16 education and training.
URL: www.lsda.org.uk

Site name: LifeBytes
Description: Website for 11–14 year olds providing facts and information
                about their health.
URL: www.lifebytes.gov.uk

Site name: Literacy: The Standards Site
Description: Support for teachers and educational professionals to
                improve literacy in schools.
URL: www.standards.dfes.gov.uk/primary/literacy

Site name: National Vocational Qualifications
Description: Information on NVQs and the career opportunities they
                provide.
URL: www.dfes.gov.uk/nvq

Site name: Numeracy: The Standards Site
Description: Support for teachers and educational professionals to
                improve numeracy in schools.
URL: www.standards.dfes.gov.uk/primary/mathematics

Site name: Practical Research for Education
Description: Online journal for education students, teachers and educa-
                tion lecturers. Includes: free articles, profile interviews with
                researchers and a forum to discuss educational research.
URL: www.pre-online.co.uk

Site name: Primary National Strategy
Description: Support from the DCSF for all aspects of primary teaching.
URL: www.standards.dfes.gov.uk/primary

Site name: Qualifications and Curriculum Authority (QCA)
Description: Website of the QCA, the governing body who maintain and develop the school curriculum and assessments and accredit and monitor qualifications.
URL: www.qca.org.uk

Site name: School Lookup
Description: Access to the DCSF EduBase database of all nurseries, schools and colleges in the UK.
URL: www.easea.co.uk

Site name: SEN
Description: Special Educational Needs page from Teachernet offering information on SEN, including materials for teachers, parents and other education professionals.
URL: www.dfes.gov.uk/sen

Site name: Standards Site
Description: Internet materials and services aiming to support and improve teacher ability and raise levels of achievement.
URL: www.standards.dfes.gov.uk

Site name: Teachernet
Description: Education website for teachers and school managers, setting the government standard for UK teachers and schools-related professions.
Including resources, lesson plans and assessment strategies.
URL: www.teachernet.gov.uk/

Site name: Teachers' Pension Scheme
Description: Information about the Teachers' Pensions Scheme for England and Wales.
URL: www.teacherspensions.co.uk/

Site name: Teacher Xpress
Description: Resources and links to educational websites covering every area of the curriculum.
URL: www.teacherxpress.com

Site name: Times Educational Supplement
Description: Jobs, resources and ideas for all teachers and people
                working in education. Resource Bank section includes a
                large section of resources for teachers by teachers.
URL: www.tes.co.uk

References

ATL	www.atl.org.uk
BBC.co.uk	www.bbc.co.uk/health/
British Dyslexia Association	www.bdadyslexia.org.uk
DCSF	www.dcsf.gov.uk
Directgov	www.direct.gov.uk
Educational Resources.co.uk	www.educationalresources.co.uk
GTC England	www.gtce.org.uk
GTC Northern Ireland	www.gtcni.org.uk
GTTR	www.gttr.ac.uk
Info Scotland: Teaching in Scotland	www.teachinginscotland.com
NASUWT	www.nasuwt.org.uk
National Autistic Society	www.autism.org.uk
NUT	www.teachers.org.uk
Scottish Credit and Qualifications Network	www.scqf.org.uk
Scottish Executive Education Department	www.scotland.gov.uk/Topics/Education
Teachernet	www.teachernet.gov.uk
EIS	www.eis.org.uk
TDA	www.tda.gov.uk
TUC	www.tuc.org.uk
UCU	www.ucu.org.uk
Voice	www.voicetheunion.org.uk

Index